BRAVE FAITH *for* HARD THINGS

Sacred Purpose in Ordinary Suffering

A Devotional by

MICHELE HOWE

Fort Washington, PA 19034

Brave Faith for Hard Things

Published by CLC Publications

USA: P.O. Box 1449, Fort Washington, PA 19034
www.clcpublications.com

UK: Kingsway CLC Trust
Unit 5, Glendale Avenue, Sandycroft, Flintshire, CH5 2QP
www.equippingthechurch.com

Printed in the United States of America

ISBN (paperback): 978-1-61958-422-8
ISBN (ebook): 978-1-61958-423-5

Italics in Scripture quotations are the emphasis of the author.

PRAISE FOR
BRAVE FAITH *for* HARD THINGS

"Michele's book speaks volumes to the discouraged, and encourages her readers to say 'yes' when everything feels like 'no.' It's trusting God in seasons of doubt and facing the unknown challenges that come along with faith! In Genesis 18:14, the Lord said to Sarah, 'Is there anything too hard for the Lord?' Once again, Michele has pointed us in the right direction: to rely on God when facing hard things, as He walks us through and gives us hope and a future."

— Nancy Sabato
Producer & Host of *The Call with Nancy Sabato*

"Michele Howe steps courageously into the truth that believers are not exempt from the trials of life. Equipped with the wisdom of her own experience with hard things, she speaks with compassion and biblical clarity in this collection of thirty devotional readings. Her message is clear: By faith we look to God's past provision, commit each new day to Him, and then trust Him for grace to face the future with courage. Each chapter reinforces the reader's hope in Jesus's two-part promise found in John 16:33. Yes, 'in this world you will have tribulation,' but never forget Part 2: Jesus said, "I have overcome the world.'"

— Michele Morin
Bible teacher, writer, and blessed grandmother

"If you struggle with life's 'hard things,' prepare to be heartened by Michele Howe's approach to the trials that come to us all. Inspired by a woman who was suffering yet held to God's promise to be with her, Michele expands on Deuteronomy 31:6 in a way that will bolster your faith and show you how to apply it to whatever you are facing."

— Judy Roberts
Writer and Journalist

"When life grows complicated with the weight of family tensions, fractured friendships, physical strain, financial pressure, and wavering faith, *Brave Faith for Hard Things* offers faith-filled direction. This interactive companion walks readers through disappointment, disillusionment, and doubt, trading reaction for renewal. With pastoral clarity and practical guidance, author Michele Howe charts a proven pathway toward resting in God's faithful, loving care. Exchange anxiety and overwhelm for hope and help in God, trusting in His promise that He is always present."

— PeggySue Wells
Award-winning, *USA Today* bestselling author of 45 books,
including *The Ten Best Decisions A Single Mom Can Make*

Brave Faith for Hard Things is a wise and steady companion for believers walking through seasons that test both heart and hope. With pastoral tenderness and biblical depth, Michele Howe invites readers to face life's hardest moments without denial or despair, anchoring courage in the character of God. Each of the thirty reflections offers space to ponder, pray, and remember that suffering never has the final word. This thoughtful devotional strengthens weary faith while reminding readers that even in the hardest places, God remains present, purposeful, and trustworthy.

— Maggie Wallem Rowe
Author of *This Life We Share:*
52 Reflections on Journeying Well with God and Others

To all my beloved friends who have been faithful
to encourage me to do hard things . . .
Because God is with me.

We can do hard things because God is with us.
Deuteronomy 31:6 (paraphrase)

Contents

Acknowledgments

PUBLISHING IS AN ever-changing, dynamic industry and so once again, I'm in the most contented of professional positions because I have the privilege to be counted among the wonderful authors of CLC Publications. I am grateful to have the opportunity to partner with this fabulous team of professionals as we work together to create a resource that will make Christ known throughout the world.

Thank you, David Fessenden, as editorial director; I am so grateful for your kindness and encouragement as I put down my thoughts on how to persevere and do hard things in this hard world. My deepest appreciation and thanks to you.

To everyone else at CLC Publications, including Jim Pitman, publisher; Jeanette Littleton, editor; Amy Beevers, associate editor; Kaitlin Hakes, marketing; and Marcia Hartman, sales; each of you is so uniquely gifted in what you do to create a winning book that has eternal implications. I am astonished at how my words are transformed into a beautiful finished product for readers to hold in their hands and treasure as I do. Once again, I'm both humbled and grateful that I have been given the privilege of putting my thoughts into a resource that others will read and glean God's good hand of provision and faithful love. I have likewise offered countless prayers of thanks on behalf of all of you. I am thankful for each of you at CLC Publications.

I also want to express my kindest appreciation to Bob Hostetler who represents me at the Steve Laube Agency. Thank you, Bob, for listening to my heart's desires and standing beside me as we work to create another resource worthy of Him.

Introduction

I'M SO EXCITED TO share the biblical truths found in Scripture that help us to discover (or rediscover) that rescue from God is always close by when we need it most. Each person will face his or her own share of "hard things" in this broken and hard world as we wait for Christ's return. And we do wait . . . eagerly! But in the meantime, how does God expect us to handle all the hard things in the world at large and within our own small intimate spheres? How do we find the courage to handle the disappointments, discouragements, and difficult moments of life? By becoming intentional and purposeful in our pursuit of God.

Let's be honest. We will have to deal with hard people, hard health struggles, hard finances, hard job setbacks, hard strained relationships, hard home situations, hard painful losses, hard lonely seasons, hard, hard, hard.

So much of life is hard and Jesus told us to expect hard times in John 16:33 (ESV), "I have said these things to you, that in me you may have peace. In the world you will have tribulation. But take heart; I have overcome the world."

Although Jesus' words to His followers may, at first glance, appear gloomy and dismal, just the opposite is true. Jesus wanted His disciples (and us) to realize that though much in this world is hard, even our hardest challenges and most grievous losses are no match for His powerful and mighty reign of sovereignty.

So what does this mean to you and me? Just that God is in control of what He allows to touch our lives . . . both the very good and the very hard. Nothing slips by Him. This truth alone should bring us much comfort and consolation.

When we truly grasp the majesty and wonder of our heavenly Father and the lengths He will go to so that we are transformed into the image of His dear Son, Jesus Christ, our hard things begin to shrink and diminish. It's true. Each of our hard things is under the care and control of the One who died to redeem us from our sins and secure for us a place in heaven forever. We can be sure that God is always doing a good work in our lives—for our ultimate good and for His glory.

Nothing on earth, not even our hardest battles, can stand against His reign and rule. So as we learn to think biblically and meditate upon these wondrous truths, God will begin to work within us in ways that are stronger and more resilient than we can imagine. He will be with us through every valley, fighting alongside us as we battle through our hard things. No place exists on earth where God isn't present and actively working on our behalf. Glory be!

So as we begin this study on learning how to overcome our hard things one faith-driven step at a time, let us thank God for His promises of faithfulness, grace, power, goodness, and nearness through it all. What a mighty God we serve!

1

We Can Do Hard Things Because Our God Is With Us

We can do hard things because God is with us.
Deuteronomy 31:6 (paraphrase)

I heard a telling statement from a dear woman whom I personally witnessed going through a series of unrelenting trials and severe suffering for five years. I took note. Her words were simple, straightforward and hit their mark squarely within my heart: "My friends have been encouraging me to do hard things because God has promised to be with me."

My gut reaction was: *What? This poor gal has been through so much already, and now her friends are encouraging her to do hard things? Her whole current life has been overrun by hard things.*

At first, I didn't know if I believed her friends were being insensitive or simply ignorant of what she had already endured.

As I later contemplated my friend's remark, something deep within me shifted. I then started to understand the wisdom of this statement and why her good friends might suggest it.

Every one of us is up against "hard things" in our lives. None of us is, or ever will be, exempt. That's why gaining a biblical understanding of how doing hard things equips us to face down even the most difficult and trying circumstances and seasons makes sense. That is, it makes sense if you are a Christian and have placed your trust in the saving work of Jesus Christ, who promises to make all things new.

As I considered this faithful believer's comments about doing hard things, I realized I should think—and do—the same. Over and over, I revisit this specific pronouncement of faith and think about how she was purposing to step out one act of courage at a time. I realized that she was determined to not allow her recent losses to hinder her effectiveness in serving Christ. Nor was she willing to sit endlessly in her grief, paralyzed by her sorrow.

Instead, I had the privilege over the following weeks and months to observe her make choices that were indeed hard. She took God at His word, and she repeatedly stepped out in faith, trusting that God would be with her every step of the way.

To hear her retell her stories, God was with her every moment of every day—even on those especially scary days when she knew that unless God upheld and strengthened her, she would not succeed. God was there providing grace, strength, and courage for her to move forward.

Although it may seem counterintuitive to step out in faith during difficult seasons when we barely are keeping our heads above water, it actually is the perfect time to do so. How so? In those vulnerable moments when we feel weary and utterly undone by the trials surrounding us, we more clearly understand the truth.

We are not ever, in and of ourselves, able to cope with, face down, or handle life-altering events in our own strength. But during those moments of desperation in life, we come to understand the full depth of our need for a Savior, a Sustainer, and a Supplier of our needs.

Only then do we cry out in abject humility and need to our gracious heavenly Father. And He hears our cry and comes close. God is with us as we turn to face our hard things.

This was where my friend discovered how God was building a new faith history in her life. She recognized that even in the midst of her hardship and suffering, God was calling her to trust Him, to lean on Him, and to follow Him wherever He called.

Like with so many of the teachings of Jesus, we come to understand that God's way of doing things is almost always opposite to our human way of thinking. Only when we learn to see with our spiritual eyes and put the full weight of our trust in God do we begin to see that He moves in the supernatural and that we can trust Him to do hard things . . . because God is with us.

My Heart's Cry

Father, I am stepping out into the scary unknown but I also am confident that You will be with me. Thank You for Your eternal promise to always be with me. Knowing that I am never alone or on my own makes all the difference. Help me to keep my eyes on You today. Give me Your grace, Your strength, and a real awareness of Your presence as I step out in faith. I know You are calling me to do hard things. I also know I cannot do so without the supernatural enabling of the Holy Spirit. Thank You for promising me Your consistent care and Your unconditional love today and always. Amen.

We Can Do Hard Things

1. *Find hope and help in God's past provision.* Take a look back and thank God for how He lovingly met your needs when you felt sorrow, grief, and pain during hard seasons. Write down a few of these memories in your journal to remind yourself of His uniquely designed, loving care for you.
2. *Find hope and help in God's present provision.* Today, take some time to reflect upon any burdens or worrisome fears you may be battling. Ask God to help you trust Him with

every concern, great or small. As you pray, remind yourself of God's promises to never leave or forsake you, as you step out to do hard things for Him.

3. *Find hope and help in God's future provision.* Spend time alone with God this week in silence, asking Him to renew your weary heart with His peace, joy, and a fresh measure of courage. Then give thanks for the eternal truth that God takes the impossible and makes it possible for our good and His glory.

2

Immeasurably More than We Ask or Imagine

Now to him who is able to do immeasurably more than all we ask or imagine, according to his power that is at work within us, to him be glory in the church and in Christ Jesus throughout all generations, forever and ever! Amen.

Ephesians 3:20–21

EVERYONE WOULD probably agree that since COVID–19 hit some years ago, everything has shifted in our world. From local to worldwide; our personal health, our social environments, our vocational work, our political worldviews, our evangelical church models all changed to accommodate this virus. Even now, though COVID–19 isn't the first consideration of the day or the first thought in our minds, life on planet Earth has changed.

Life seems to have shifted and continues to do so at an alarmingly swift rate of speed. While we cannot compare changes in our individual lives to the worldwide upheaval that occurred during the early COVID–19 years, we still feel the residual stress from that difficult time. Its aftermath lingers and continues to impact us in secondary ways. It may not frighten us, but it affects us and our families, our colleagues, and our church families.

As we consider the immense pressure all of us were under as we attempted to navigate those difficult days, I wonder how much internal stress and pressure we continue to feel even today? While some still face challenges from the coronavirus disaster, others were already feeling the distress of other traumas in life. When we think of pain of the past, most of us simply want to move forward. And yet, there always remains a just-under-the-surface reminder of our past pain and internal angst.

So how do we move forward in the present when we continue to feel the scars of the past? Some people face the scars of childhood trauma or a terminal diagnosis or a job loss or a divorce or a death or . . .

The list can go on and on and on. Whatever our battle scars may be (and we all have them), how do we take stock of our losses and move into the future with grit and grace?

It's simple; but it's not easy. We learn to take God at His word. We learn to bank on God's promises of perfect provision no matter what we are facing.

But perhaps most of all, we learn to know how wondrous and glorious our heavenly Father is. Because as we get to know God's unchanging, magnificent character, we learn we can trust Him with anything (and anything means everything).

So today, though we may be battle-weary and war-torn, we can do our next thing—our next hard thing. Consider this powerful promise we read in Ephesians 3: We can count on God to do what we cannot accomplish. We can be confident in God's supernatural supply of grace and strength to carry out whatever task or responsibility He asks of us. We can rest in His faithful, loving care for us, even during the hardest seasons of life.

Yes, God does promise to do immeasurably more than we ask or imagine. Consider that! God will do way more than we can ask of Him . . . or even imagine. It's almost too good to be true. But it is true because God said it, and God does not lie.

Because of the power that is working within us God readies us with what we require to accomplish His will for our lives. God is in the business of transforming the worst of the worst into something glorious and eternally redeemable.

So today, if you feel completely undone and weary by life's trials, go to God. Ask Him to renew your strength. Ask Him to give you a fresh measure of His hope, joy, and peace. Then prayerfully take that next step, because you know God will supply all your needs as you face hard things in your life today.

My Heart's Cry

Father, I am so worn out from this seemingly unending season of trials. I am weary beyond belief and simply want it to end. But I also know You are the one who promises to meet my every need. You alone can bring sanity to our crazy world. You alone supply hope, joy, and peace. Lord, fill me anew with these spiritual gifts, and give me the strength I need to step out in faith. I must face the hard things in my life and I can only do so with Your enabling grace and strength. Amen.

We Can Do Hard Things

1. *Find hope and help in God's past provision.* Spend time reflecting upon seasons when you felt uncertain and afraid about your life and the state of the world. Ask God to help you remember how He rescued you, how He resolved hard issues, and how He transformed these difficulties into something beautiful to behold.
2. *Find hope and help in God's present provision.* Today, ask God to show you specific ways in which He is meeting your needs one day at a time. Thank Him for these reminders of His

persistent love toward you even when life is hard and the way ahead is unclear. Praise Him for His new-morning mercies that are everyday evidences of His continued sovereign reign over all of life.

3. *Find hope and help in God's future provision.* Before you begin your day, pray and ask God to calm any fears, settle any worries, and take away any anxiety about the future. Ask Him to fill your heart with His perfect peace and then give Him thanks for the good work He is doing in your heart and life. Bless the Lord and with praise and thanksgiving because you know the God you serve is worthy of your trust even when life is full of hard things.

3

Saying "Yes" When We Want to Say "No"

And I heard the voice of the Lord saying,
"Whom shall I send, and who will go for us?"
Then I said, "Here am I! Send me."

Isaiah 6:8, ESV

MY DEAR FRIEND of many years received a phone call—well, she received many calls, to be accurate. Each one was unwanted. But the fact remained; each call was a call for help. So as a faithful sister in the Lord and a biblical counselor, she answered that call.

This particular call was a cry for help from a woman in dire need of solid biblical truth, hope, and help. Thank the good Lord that someone sent this hurting woman to my godly friend to provide the spiritual guidance and support she so desperately needed.

Still, the fact remained that my wonderful friend didn't want to answer this call . . . not on that day—nor at any time in the foreseeable future. Why? Because she, herself, was in the throes of a difficult family crisis and she didn't feel she had the wisdom, strength, or stamina to give anything of value to anyone else at this time. But she was wrong.

In truth, we are all mistaken when we believe that we cannot offer something eternally beneficial to another person when our own call to help arrives. The truth is: We never accomplish anything of eternal value in our own strength. We do so only if the Lord supplies exactly what we require when we lend a hand, offer a word of encouragement, and provide a new reason to hope.

How often do we do just what my friend felt like doing? We are all tempted to say "no" when the Lord is nudging us to say "yes." I can recount numerous times when I felt completely done-in and ill-equipped to offer anything remotely beneficial to someone else. And yet at times, by faith alone, I said "yes" anyway and entered a situation with fear and trembling.

And we all know what comes next, right? God in His kindness and mercy met me in that place of utter dependence upon Him alone.

In short, God had me right where He wanted me. Dependent. Weak. Needy. Fully aware that unless He supplied me with the resources I needed to make a difference, it wouldn't happen.

Oh how the Lord must feel bemused by His dear children in these situations. Every part of our being can be screaming, "No, no, no—not now (if ever)." And still the Lord gently urges us to say that difficult "yes" because He always knows what is ahead. He is in the business of orchestrating all of life. Surely, God can give us what we need in the small and mundane service we offer to others.

But let's be honest. Truth be told, we hate feeling dependent and weak and needy. Don't we? Many years ago I read an account by Elizabeth Elliot who wrote that every believer wants to serve from a position of power and wellness and strength. But this is usually not what happens in this hard, broken, and imperfect world.

If we are being completely transparent, most of the time we feel just the opposite. We are not in positions of power. We are not feeling our best. We are not strong and mighty. And still, God calls us to do our hard things because He is with us. And in the grand scheme of life eternal, that is truly all that matters. We can do hard things, even in our weakest, most vulnerable moments, because our God is with us.

Back to my dear friend's dilemma. She did indeed answer that call. She discovered that our God who calls us is also the One who supplies our every need, even when we don't feel up to the challenge, whatever it may be. God promises to be with us; He promises to give us His divine wisdom, grace, and strength.

He gives this to us one day at time. No matter how daunting our life circumstances may be today, we can do the hard things God is calling us to do. Why? Because He promises to be with us. Amen and amen.

My Heart's Cry

Father, here I am again, feeling weak and overwhelmed by life and all its responsibilities. Help me to put the full weight of my trust in You alone. Remind me that You are my sole provider and the only help I need. Give me the wisdom I require to know when to say "yes" and when to say "no." Lord, I need Your guidance every day . . . every hour. Show me that You are always before me, behind me, and beside me through each day. I want to faithfully serve You and others, but I need Your moment-by-moment enabling. Thank You, Lord. Amen.

We Can Do Hard Things

1. *Find hope and help in God's past provision.* When you awaken each morning this week, spend a few moments calling to mind how God met your every need in times past. Specifically recall seasons when you felt weak and overwhelmed. Then remember how God intervened and strengthened you.

2. *Find hope and help in God's present provision.* Today prayerfully contemplate what responsibilities lie before you and pray specifically for each one. Ask God to give you His divine wisdom and understanding. Then thank Him in advance for His mighty powerful provision that He has promised to every believer.
3. *Find hope and help in God's future faithfulness.* As you pray about the coming days, be specific, asking God to enable you to live one day at a time in complete peace, joy, and contentment. Come what may, ask the Lord to fill your heart and mind with His bountiful promises to take care of you, guard you, and supply your every need.

4

Stopping Fear in Its Tracks

You have searched me, Lord, and you know me. You know when I sit and when I rise; you perceive my thoughts from afar. You discern my going out and my lying down; you are familiar with all my ways. Before a word is on my tongue you, Lord, know it completely. You hem me in behind and before, and you lay your hand upon me.

Psalm 139:1–5

CHANGE. NO ONE likes it. We may believe we love change when it's something we have been praying for and praying about . . . let's say, a new job, a new baby, a new friendship, a new start, and on and on.

But let's be honest. When change of any type begins to happen, we tend to tense up and get stressed out.

When my firstborn daughter announced she was going to have a baby I was thrilled. Until I wasn't. Suddenly, all the past parental responsibilities and stresses that come along with parenting began to rear up in my memory. Even though I wasn't having another child, I started to recall everything that parenting a child involves, and I felt overwhelmed.

I didn't stay in this anxious space for long. However, I recall feeling somewhat nervous about my coming role as a new grandmother, and I felt inadequate. Why? Because I gave way to all the "what ifs" and "how can we" questions. Everything that could possibly go wrong started to erupt within my mind. That's not a good place to be when you only want to express delight and joyful winsomeness about your future grandchild's appearance.

How often do we react in the same way when we receive unexpected news, whether of the good or hard variety? We are human, finite beings. We are not in control, as much as we would like to be. We are not the masters of our fate . . . ever.

It's simple. When we receive news of any type of life change, it can paralyze us in fear.

God doesn't want this reaction for us. Our gracious heavenly Father wants us to learn how to receive life's changes with the good grace and confident trust that He is so worthy of and deserves.

As Psalm 139 says, God already knows us, He knows when we sit and when we rise, He knows our very thoughts and words before we think or utter a single syllable. He watches us closely as we are going out and when we lie down. He is intimately familiar with everything about us.

But perhaps the very best part of these comforting verses is that God hems us in both behind and before, and He lays His hand upon us.

Think about it. Our gracious and oh, so great heavenly Father not only surrounds us with His love and protection, but He is already in our future. Wherever our foot steps, God is already there.

He knows the way we will take. He knows our heart's fears, worries, and concerns. And He has compassion on all He has made. Our God loves to love us. Our God loves to strengthen and encourage us. Our God surrounds us with His mighty right hand. Our God will enable us to face our fears, whatever they may be. Our God reigns sovereignly over all of the heavens and the earth.

The more we understand about our magnificent God, the easier we will find it to rest when change arrives on our front doorstep. Remember, our gracious heavenly Father is already in our future.

My Heart's Cry

Father, I feel as though everything—and I do mean everything—in my life is shifting and shaking. From relationships, to health, to work, to family dynamics, to church fellowship and service. Every thing feels like just too much. Please help me to find my comfort and my sole consolation in my relationship with You alone. Help me to understand that Your absolute sovereignty is Your way of guiding and directing my path. Show me Your goodness today and grant me a willing heart to surrender all to You. Clothe me with a humble, submissive, and teachable heart today and every day. Come what may, give me the grace to keep my eyes on You alone. Amen.

We Can Do Hard Things

1. *Find hope and help in God's past provision.* Look back to past seasons when you felt overwhelmed and afraid of the future. Then prayerfully spend some time recording specific events and how God met you in your place of fear and uncertainty. Next, locate a Bible verse that describes how God provided for you in just the right way that met your needs perfectly.
2. *Find hope and help in God's present provision.* Focus on any changes that are taking place in your life now. Ask the Lord to give you His perfect peace about each different scenario. Then spend time praying that God will open your eyes to see these changes as bountiful blessings from His hand. Pray that God will show you how He is pouring goodness into your life

as you walk into this new and fresh season. Then journal your honest thoughts and concerns about these changes.

3. *Find hope and help in God's future provision.* As you talk to God about the future, spend time in praise and worship before you pour out your concerns and worries. Remind yourself of God's magnificence, His sovereignty, and His perfect rule over the heavens and the earth. Speak the biblical truth that God has promised to meet your every need, and our God does not lie. Give Him the thanks and praise He is so worthy of, and then ask Him to strengthen your faith. Sit before God and give thanks that no matter where your foot steps in this life, He is already there.

5

Our Weaknesses Are Not Hindrances

As a father shows compassion to his children, so the LORD shows compassion to those who fear him. For he knows our frame; he remembers that we are dust.

Psalm 103:13–14, ESV

WHEN MY FRIEND told me she had terminal cancer, I cried. When another friend said her spouse had left her, I cried. When my daughter told me her family was moving across the state, and my son told me at the same time that he was moving across the country, I cried. When I realized my sweet mom had dementia, I cried. When I received bad health news, I cried.

Our life is fraught with hard things, isn't it? Those hard things arrive in all sorts of sizes, from miniscule to the mighty-big and completely overwhelming.

And let's be honest, generally speaking, what is our first response to hard news? We respond with fear and quaking, right? We hone in on our weakness and frailty. We then figuratively melt on the inside when we hear about the difficult and oh-so-hard things that our loved ones are enduring. We feel inadequate to face all these hard things even when—maybe even especially when—we are not the ones suffering, but those we care about are in the throes of their own heartbreaking seasons.

This is why we must hone the wise art of learning to reframe these hard things into a heavenly perspective that places total confidence in God. As Psalm 103 tells us, God knows our frame. He remembers that we are dust.

This very statement brings me great comfort and joy. Why? Because I am keenly aware of my weakness and frailty—my inability to handle the hard things in life in my own strength. I know how much I need my heavenly Father's compassion and His hour-by-hour sustaining grace and strength to see me through the day.

God's Word is clear about the suffering and hardship we will have to endure this side of heaven. Hard news, right? Yet, God's Word also assures us that when we see Jesus, all of our pain, sorrow, grief, and suffering will end forever. This promise of eternal communion with God—minus all the earthly suffering that surrounds us on every side—is crucial for us to internalize and set our heart and mind upon each day.

Every single day, we will face hard things, and every single day we will come face-to-face with our weaknesses, frailty, and inability to endure these trials outside of the power of God's indwelling Holy Spirit who teaches us, comforts us, and lives within us.

Our weaknesses are not hindrances; they are an invitation to greater intimacy and communion with God. But to reach that place of closeness with Him, we have to invest ourselves in knowing Him through His Word.

When we neglect reading and studying God's Word, we handicap the Holy Spirit, because He cannot bring to our mind what we haven't first ingested and meditated upon. What a powerful reminder to delve deeply into God's Word daily for our required spiritual, mental, and emotional renewal so we can view our hard things through the lens of eternity.

Today's believer is no different than any of the biblical heroes of the faith. Those men and women were as vulnerable to failure and sin as we are today. They faltered and fell as we do.

But unlike them, we get to observe through the Old and New Testament's recounting of these historical individuals how God met them in their place of great need and provided a way of escape, protection, healing, and rescue from whatever hard things they had to endure.

So today, when your life seems full to overflowing with hard things, and you feel anything but robust, sturdy, and strong, meditate on this psalm. Remind yourself that God knows you are but dust, and He has great compassion on you. Then remember that your weaknesses do not hinder our great God, who promises to supply everything we need to serve and obey Him.

My Heart's Cry

Father, today I feel so weak and frail. I feel completely inadequate to face the hard things before me. If I'm honest, I want run and hide away from my responsibilities and tasks. Help me, Lord, to remember that You know my weaknesses, and You know that I am but dust. My frame was created by You and designed by Your mighty hand. Give me the wisdom to put the full weight of my trust into Your capable hands, because You have promised to meet me where I am and to supply my every need. Let me be comforted by the truth that You know how needy I am, and You have compassion on me. Thank You, Father, for always being near to me and for hearing my heart's cry whenever I pray. Amen.

We Can Do Hard Things

1. *Find hope and help in God's past provision.* Note the seasons in the past when you felt completely helpless and inadequate to fulfill the responsibilities before you. Then remember (with gratitude) how God stepped in to meet you in that hard place

and supplied you with everything you needed. Thank Him today for His faithful and compassionate care for you in days gone by.

2. *Find hope and help in God's present faithfulness.* Today, spend time alone with the Lord in prayer, and ask Him to calm any anxiety you may experience. Ask God to give you joy, hope, and peace that will reign supreme in your heart, no matter what foe you may face. Then say His name—Jesus, the name above all names—again and again and again.
3. *Find hope and help in God's future faithfulness.* Even if you believe your future is uncertain because of your suffering, remind yourself that God has promised to never leave or forsake you. He has promised He will supply your every need, and that includes supernatural grace to face any foe. Search Scripture for verses that define God's unchanging character, and meditate on who God says He is. Your troubles will diminish as you focus on the greatness of our God.

6

Focus On God's Mighty, Enabling Power

Finally, brothers and sisters, whatever is true, whatever is noble, whatever is right, whatever is pure, whatever is lovely, whatever is admirable—if anything is excellent or praiseworthy—think about such things.

Philippians 4:8

THROUGH A SERIES of major life shifts, someone dear to me faced multi-faceted changes and life upsets. Her husband took a new job across the state, which meant their moving from their home, their lifelong friends, their church, and their extended family. In every way imaginable, my friend's life was altering in ways that she felt were insurmountable to accept.

She talked about how difficult it had been to decide to switch jobs during such a busy season of life for their entire young family. But they had prayed, and they had sought biblical counsel.

In short, this couple believed they made the wisest decision for the long-term health and well-being of their family. But that was then. Now, in the midst of these exhausting life transitions, she wonders if they had made a mistake.

Let's face it: Whenever we make a major life decision, we can lose everything comfortable and familiar. As my friend discovered, trying to find a new grocery store, a nearby post office, trusted physicians, an excellent school, and on and on was a big deal. My dear one didn't want "new"; she longed for well-acquainted and reliable. Don't we all?

Soon she discovered something that helped her handle her own set of hard circumstances. My friend eventually realized she was focusing on everything she needed to do to make her family comfortable; however she failed to position her thoughts first and foremost on God and who He is. She realized in her good desire to see her family quickly settled in their new home, she ended up burdened under a load too heavy to bear.

Wisely, my dear friend began to shift her focus onto God and His mighty, enabling power, which she read about in the Bible. She purposefully started to focus on Him rather than on her long to-do list. She also began to obey God's mandate from Philippians 4 where the apostle Paul told us to think about what is true, what is noble, what is right, what is pure, what is lovely, what is admirable, what is excellent, and what is praiseworthy.

The more disciplined she became in making this thoughtful exercise a daily practice, the more her spirit soared instead of plummeting. As missionary and author Elizabeth Elliot once noted, sometimes life gets so hard you can only do the next thing. My friend made her next thing to focus on God and His goodness. In slow and steady increments, all the difficult things that weighed her down started to dissipate and lose their power to paralyse and defeat her.

When we choose to place our thoughts on God first, even life's most daunting challenges can begin to diminish. It's as though in the face of God's mighty, enabling power, all other foes start to fade away.

Since we know from Scripture that we serve a mighty God, how can we not run to Him for refuge and strength when life's demands bring us low?

Still, too often our first response (or second, third, and so on) is not to run to Him, who is the only One who has the power and the desire to help us. No, we falter and fail as we struggle in our own puny strength until we realize at last that God is our only resource in good times and hard times. But what a wonderful realization this is when God brings us to this point of reckoning, when we understand He truly is our all in all.

My Heart's Cry

Father, I am feeling tired with everything I need to accomplish. I am overwhelmed, and I don't believe this load of responsibilities will ever ease up. I'm trying my best to serve my family and do all I can to make our new life more stable and comfortable. It's been a truly emotional and tiresome season. Oh, Lord, hear my prayer. Help me to shift my heavy thoughts from all that is before me onto You. Help me to remember who You are! Help me to focus on Your mighty, enabling power every hour of my day. And Lord, give me the strength to redirect my thoughts to everything good, as described in Philippians 4. Thank You for sustaining me and for loving me so dearly. Amen.

We Can Do Hard Things

1. *Find hope and help in God's past provision.* Take time to remember what God has done for you in the past. Specifically recall moments when life felt like too much to bear and when your responsibilities were so burdensome you wanted to give up. Then give thanks for how God met you in your time of need.
2. *Find hope and help in God's present provision.* Today, instead of dreading the day's tasks and responsibilities, thank God for

His promised wisdom, guidance, and provision. Write down any specific tasks that overwhelm you. Then look up several verses that bring you comfort and hope, and meditate on these powerful truths. Use Philippians 4 as your grid for right thinking, and then give thanks to God for each of these blessings from His hand. Put your hope in God's mighty, enabling power—not in your own strength.

3. *Find hope and help in God's future provision.* As you look ahead to the coming weeks and months, do not let the busyness or potential stressful seasons overwhelm you with dread. Flip that switch by choosing to focus on God first. Then discipline yourself to work through Philippians 4 a portion at a time by lingering in the specific goodness that the Lord has infused into your life.

7

When Our Faith Has to Step Up to the Plate

Even though I walk through the valley of the shadow of death, I will fear no evil, for you are with me; your rod and your staff, they comfort me.

Psalm 23:4, ESV

RECENTLY, OUR pastor taught from Acts 13, describing Paul's journey to reach the Gentiles. He commented that people often remark, "Life is a journey" in a cheesy sort of way.

But that is true. Life is a journey. However, as finite humans, we frequently spout off these trite sayings without truly realizing the spiritual implications of such statements. If we honestly understand that as God's beloved children, we are literally journeying through this finite life to our never-ending eternal life, how should we be living today?

Further, our pastor challenged us to seriously consider—with much prayer and self-inspection—how much of the world has affected, or even infected, our hearts and minds, and thus, our lifestyle. The world has influenced all of us in major proportions, and the daily choices we make reveal this fact.

God's challenge to me was this: Am I in earnest when I say that I want God's will above my own? Am I willing to live one day at a time, setting aside my preferences so I can be an encouragement and blessing to another? Am I ready to sacrifice what I hold most dear if God calls me to do so? Am I? Are you?

These are difficult questions to ask ourselves. But we must. Even today, as I sit writing on this challenging topic of letting go of what I most desire, I am wrestling internally with worries and all the unknowns that the future will bring. This is when I have to start talking back to my thoughts and let my faith step up to the plate.

One of my favorite psalms is Psalm 23 because it reckons with all of life's challenges and stages. The fourth verse tells me that even the very worst that can come at me is eternally the best. Even when I am scared stiff by some hard circumstance in my life, I can get to a place of perfect peace and truly fear no evil. Why? Because Jesus promised to be with me—in the furnace, in the fire, on the raging sea, and in the lowest valley. Jesus' faithful love reigns supreme over every circumstance and situation.

Jesus will also use His rod and staff to guide me through these difficult terrains, and their effective protective use will comfort me. God uses both the good and bad to display His wondrous love for each of us. He demonstrates His perfect—and always present—intimate care for every one of His children, through the means of discipline and guidance. Yes, even when we have fallen into grievous sin, our God stands ready to forgive and restore us.

Because He walks with us, we find our strength to move through the dimmest seasons of life, even when our emotions are numb, our bodies are failing, our minds are confused, and our spirits are discouraged. When we are flailing around for relief from pain, we are more prone to look to Him. When we fail in multiple areas of our lives, we are most likely to look up to Him.

When our hopes and dreams have died, when our family and friends are suffering beyond belief, when we are losing hope by the minute, we look to Him in quiet desperation.

Perhaps during these hard, hard seasons, God does His greatest work of transformation in our souls. Scripture tells us this is so. But we must believe it is true by praying through these dark times with hearts full of faith . . . even when—especially when—circumstances make no earthly sense and our faith wavers.

God is with us. God will sustain us. God will guide and comfort us—and we need not fear any evil.

My Heart's Cry

Father, today is yet another reminder of how weak and frail I am. I am surrounded by daunting circumstances, both up close and personal and from a distance. Everywhere I look, I see suffering and pain. It feels like such a dark time for everyone I love. Please, Lord, draw near to me in such a way that I am aware of Your loving presence even now. I need You, Father. I need Your loving hand to guide and strengthen. I need Your Spirit to comfort me and to teach me. Precious, Lord, I want to trust You with my very life; help me to lay it down every morning when I arise. And every evening when I lay down to sleep, remind me of Your wondrous work in my life and throughout the entire world. Amen.

We Can Do Hard Things

1. *Find hope and help in God's past provision.* This week, reflect on God's great work of guidance and care for you in the past. Prayerfully, ask the Lord to remind you of those times when you felt alone, lost, and afraid. Then begin thanking Him for His carefully executed love toward you that sustained and strengthened you during that hard season. Never forget God's goodness to you, and then thank Him for it.

2. *Find hope and help in God's present provision.* Today, ask the Lord to give you exactly what you need to meet the challenges before you with fierce faith and robust hope. Remind yourself of this psalm that speaks of God's presence even in the darkest valley. Remember that God will use both His rod and His staff to rebuke, guide, and comfort you. Thank Him for His perfect plan for your life and how it will echo into eternity.
3. *Find hope and help in God's future provision.* If you feel afraid of coming days that are filled with scary unknowns and frightening uncertainties, ask God to shield your heart and mind from these nameless fears. Then take steps to replace your fearful thoughts with faith-driven promises. Spend time locating and writing down specific verses that build your confidence in our true and faithful God. Carry these powerful promises with you throughout your day.

8

Become Friends with Feeling Uncomfortable

But solid food is for the mature, for those who have their powers of discernment trained by constant practice to distinguish good from evil.

Hebrews 5:14, ESV

FAR TOO OFTEN, we believers emphasize our feelings far too much. How we feel from one day to the next frequently determines our thoughts and our actions.

I wonder how differently we all would live if we valued what God values? Faith over fear. Obedience over emotions. Holiness over happiness.

Author Randy Alcorn has said that Christians in general place more emphasis on their happiness than on their holiness. True? Sadly, I agree with Alcorn's premise.

Not sure if you agree? Consider this barometer regarding how you make decisions. When you wake in the morning and review your responsibilities for the day, to what effect does your mood impact your day? If you feel weary and overwhelmed, do those emotions, valid though they may be, dictate if you will follow through with your commitments?

I fear most of us fall into this category where we place too much emphasis on what our current emotional temperature is at any given moment. Still not convinced? Then consider how often you speak these words, "I just don't feel like it." Or perhaps this is your excuse of choice, "Maybe later, but right now I'm not feeling it."

We all express these types of rejoinders when contemplating our next steps. And when we do, we are giving way to our ever-altering, ever-changing emotions rather than relying on the self-control and supernatural strength God promises to supply.

I love this passage from Hebrews where it exhorts us to learn, by daily practice, to discern good from evil. We are told that we are mature in our faith if we can handle the solid food that Scripture provides for believers to live by and obey.

The more we press into the Lord despite our unreliable feelings, the more we become able to discern right from wrong, good from evil, and put sound biblical principles into consistent practice. Perhaps the most common phrase we hear when someone does not want to participate in any type of hard endeavor is: "I'm just not comfortable doing that."

I've said it. You've said it. I'm pretty confident every person from the beginning of time has uttered this statement at least once. Let's be clear: Sometimes legitimate times and reasons exist expressing this sentiment. However, what a shame to use this common excuse to not step out in faith to serve God.

As we grow in our faith and mature in Christ, we must be willing to become friends with feeling uncomfortable. The longer we walk with our Lord, the more He will demand from us. Our faith will be tested. Our suffering and sorrow may increase. Our denial of our selfish desires and personal preferences will be placed on the altar so we fulfill God's plan and purpose for us.

This isn't an easy truth to bear. But our gracious heavenly Father won't allow us to stagnate in the infant stage of faith.

Instead, He will continue to position us in places where we routinely feel uncomfortable and uneasy so that His glory and goodness will shine all the brighter. So today, when we are tempted to give way to our uncomfortable feelings that paralyze us, let us instead allow the Lord to strengthen us with His glorious power and might. Let us pray for spiritual boldness and a sturdy faith that relies solely on the provision and power of our almighty God.

My Heart's Cry

Father, please help me know that You are enough for me today. Help me to develop the self-control I need so I do not give way to my ever-changing emotions. I feel uncomfortable so much of the time. In fact, sometimes I wonder what is wrong with me. Please, Lord, give me Your divine wisdom to know when to say "yes" and when to say "no" and to not let my emotions dictate my decisions. Remind me that You are always with me—closer than my next breath—and that no matter where I place my next step, You are already there. Thank You, Lord, for the good work You are already doing in my life and for what You will accomplish in and through me in the coming days. Amen.

We Can Do Hard Things

1. *Find hope and help in God's past provision.* As you reflect upon the times when your emotions took control and you felt helpless and afraid; remember how God met you in that fragile place. Note how God ministered to you even when you felt uncomfortable and unable to move forward. Look back with honesty. Did you feel paralyzed by fear? What might you have done differently to have traversed through that difficult time with a more conscious reliance upon God?

2. *Find hope and help in God's present provision.* Today when you survey what is right before you, ask yourself if God is calling you to step out in faith in any areas—but you feel reluctant to do so. Have you been invited to serve or minister in new areas of opportunity or new capacities, but you have said no? Prayerfully, come before the Lord and ask Him to reveal if you are living faithful obedience or fearful hesitation. Then ask God to provide you with the fortitude to move with His enabling strength into any of these situations you should accept.
3. *Find hope and help in God's future provision.* As you look to the future, remember God's past provision and His current provision. Shore yourself up with the faith history that God has already proved Himself faithful to you in every way. Be careful to write down these significant moments in your life when you felt overwhelmed and uncomfortable, and yet, note of how God met you in your place of neediness. Thank Him for teaching you self-control and discernment between good and evil. Be grateful today that God has promised to stay nearer than your next breath, no matter what the future holds.

9

It's Okay to Know You Are Not Enough

Be still, and know that I am God.

Psalm 46:10

IN THE AFTERMATH of the murder of a godly young man who spoke with wisdom, kindness, generosity, and love, our nation is reeling over a display of senseless evil. We cry. We pray. We turn our hearts to the only One who can bring us comfort and help us regain lost hope.

Again and again, we must choose to place our only hope in God. He alone can right the wrongs, heal the hurting, and mend the brokenhearted.

When we face the evil of this fallen world, our hearts can grow so weary of the needless sorrow, grief, and pain inflicted on the innocent. Our hearts cry out to God, as we should, because Scripture tells us to do just that. But in all our crying, sometimes we do not gain any relief from our emotional pain. Why?

I believe the peace we seek, the inner calm we long for, and the relief from the knowledge that evil is indeed all around us is this: We still mistakenly hold on to that false hope that somehow within ourselves we can stop this madness, we can stop this violence.

It's true that each of us must make wise and prudent decisions, and our choices truly do echo into eternity. However, none of us is powerful enough, influential enough, and persuasive enough to stop evil in its tracks. On this side of heaven, evil is much bigger than any—or all—of us.

This is why we need to grapple with and accept the truth that we are not enough. None of us can hinder what God has allowed. He alone has the wisdom, power, and strength to usher in the cease-and-desist of sin and all its painful repercussions that ripple throughout the world and through the ages.

This is why this specific verse in Psalm 46 is so appropriate for those critical moments when we feel we must do something to stop the suffering around us. Let us carefully read and then reread this verse, "Be still, and know that I am God."

God is speaking here as a loving, all-knowing Father to His beloved, treasured children (us). He is uttering a firm command—not a gentle pep talk or a soft request. God is commanding us to *be still.*

Think about your own father or mother or any parental figure in your life who cared about your well-being. Picture this trusted person listening to your cries, seeing your tears, and feeling the anguish of your heart. Then, imagine them looking you straight in the eye and saying, "Enough. Trust me. I will take care of this for you."

How do you respond? You visibly relax, and you literally exhale all your fears, worries, and anxieties. You know help is coming, and you can take a backseat to whatever transpires next.

This is exactly what God expects of us when we read and meditate upon this powerful passage. *Be still.* Why? *I am God.*

Here God offers us a rebuke from His loving and strong Father's heart. He is commanding us to obey Him. This isn't a verse that tells us to sip our tea lake side in the perfect calm of a colorful fall afternoon. No, this is the Almighty's righteous command for us who are dead center in a war zone.

God knows we are facing hard things, and they come in all shapes and sizes. He also knows we are never enough in and of ourselves to face these challenges in our own strength. This is why He issues this command as if He were the commander in chief of the world's fiercest army—and He is!

So today, when we reach the very end of our strength and we mourn over the escalating evil that surrounds us, let's cease and desist. Let's obey our Father and *be still* . . . because we know that He is God.

My Heart's Cry

Father, my heart is breaking today. My soul aches over senseless acts of evil and destruction. I pray that You, Lord, come quickly and end all this grievous suffering throughout the world. We feel helpless, hopeless even. How can any of us stop the forces of evil that appear to be escalating at every turn. Father, help me to draw ever closer to You and derive my comfort and strength from You alone. Please comfort all of us with Your continued presence in our lives. Watch over us and teach us what it means to be still and know that You are God. Amen.

We Can Do Hard Things

1. *Find hope and help in God's past provision.* When you begin to feel weary over the world's sinfulness and destruction, become a good rememberer. Take time to be still and simply remember all that God has done on your behalf. Ask Him to bring to your mind all those moments when you felt crushed over the sinfulness of the world. Reflect on how His new-morning mercies strengthened your heart and gave you eternal perspective.
2. *Find hope and help in God's present provision.* If you feel overcome by grief and sorrow from a present tragedy, turn

to Him with all your pain, your questions, your doubts, and your fears. Turn to God and pour your heart out before Him. Then, be still. Obey God's fatherly command to be still . . . and know that He is God. Turn your pain into prayers and watch Him work.

3. *Find hope and help in God's future provision.* As you think about, or worry about, the coming months and years, stop those thoughts that produce a repeat cycle of anxiety in your heart and mind. Turn to Scripture and drink deeply of its rich truths. Find your heart consoled and comforted by God's mighty proclamation that we can be still . . . because He is God. Be still. Know that He is God.

10

When God Calls, He Supplies Our Every Need

Take the helmet of salvation and the sword of the Spirit, which is the word of God.

Ephesians 6:17

WHEN GOD CALLS, we can rest assured that He will supply our every need. Scripture tells us this is true. But do we truly believe it?

Most of us are given an opportunity to serve the Lord, and we prayerfully consider. We say "yes" if it is possible. Then we begin to trust that the Lord will indeed orchestrate our schedules, our energy, our health, and our time so we can fulfill whatever task He has set before us.

What we do not count on is that often, God allows—perhaps even orchestrates—various obstacles to enter the picture at the same time we have committed ourselves to serve. This is indeed life on our broken planet. So how do we bravely say "yes" to those future opportunities to give of our time, talents, and gifts without entering new responsibilities with some measure of fear?

We must equip ourselves with the spiritual armor God has so graciously supplied for us. Specifically, during these hard times of testing, in which we are simultaneously required to step up and serve others, we must put on the helmet of salvation and the sword of the Spirit.

When we have confidence that we are children of the Most High, we know we can, and should, run to Him with our every need. Whether we are feeling robust or weak, energized or exhausted, rested or overwhelmed, God, as our beloved heavenly Father, expects us to talk with Him. We must tell Him through our prayers what we are thinking, feeling, and wrestle through. We must take our doubts and discouragements to Him.

Knowing we belong to Him for all eternity settles our hearts, eases our minds, and calms our emotions. For we understand that no matter how hard today may be, we are hurtling headlong into the beautiful and blessed eternity with the Creator of the heavens and the earth. That truth alone changes everything about how we choose to face down our hard things today.

Next, we must learn to wield the sword of the Spirit, which is the Word of God. This is where we find many believers fail. We say we are too busy, too tired, too distracted, too depressed, or too overwhelmed to take advantage of the power of God's Word as it applies to our lives.

Perhaps a primary tool God employs to supply our every need when He calls us to serve Him is His living and active Word. We must discipline ourselves to spend time daily reading and meditating upon God's eternal truths. This is where God meets with us up close and personal, and as He does, He speaks hope, help, courage, encouragement, and exhortation so we can serve Him effectively.

Today if you feel overwhelmed by the yeses you have said in regard to serving others, ask yourself if you are using these two primary pieces of spiritual armor. Have you thoughtfully meditated on the amazing truth that you will live with God throughout eternity as one of His precious own children? And if so, how can you neglect learning all you can about your heavenly Father through the careful study of His Word? Not one of us is strong enough to neglect either of these essential pieces of spiritual armor.

God has promised to meet our every need for every situation. But He has also called us to avail ourselves of the security of our salvation by understanding with full effect what it means to become a child of God. And then, we must grow into diligent students of God's very Word through daily reading, prayer, and mediation.

We cannot complain to God about a lack of resources to fulfill our tasks if we neglect the powerful resources He has placed at our disposal. Hard things will always come our way. Hard times truly are the norm in this hard world. But God has provided all we require to love and serve Him, despite the brokenness of this sin-ridden, temporary realm.

My Heart's Cry

Father, I said "yes" to new opportunities to serve You. As soon as I did so, it seemed as though everything began to unravel at home and in my personal life. My time is not my own because I am responsible for my family and other tasks that no one else can take on. Help me, Lord. I feel overwhelmed. Please help me to reframe these new difficulties in light of eternity. Give me Your wisdom to grasp that hard times are indeed temporary. Remind me that You have promised to supply my every need in every circumstance. And Lord, strengthen my resolve to spend more time in Your Word every day so that when life becomes too hard, I can rest in Your precious promises and find comfort and peace there. Amen.

We Can Do Hard Things

1. *Find hope and help in God's past provision.* As you reflect upon your past, ask the Lord to help you recall moments when you were called upon to love and serve others in the midst of

your own hard season of life. Remind yourself how burdened you felt and then ask yourself some hard questions. Did you avail yourself of the comfort and consolation of being one of God's own beloved children? And did you diligently spend time daily in God's Word—reading, praying, and mediating upon its life-changing truths?

2. *Find hope and help in God's present provision.* Today, as you begin your day, be honest with God. Pour your heart out to Him. Ask Him to give you everything you need to love and serve others today. Then ask God to help you keep your thoughts on this day alone, for we only have today, and He has promised His strength and grace one day at a time. Thank God for the salvation of your eternal soul. Thank Him for His holy Word which prepares you to go out into the world as a light reflecting Jesus.
3. *Find hope and help in God's future provision.* Spend time asking God to direct your path. Ask Him to give you fresh opportunities to love and serve others, as well as the strength and stamina to do so. Consider what a great God we serve, and don't neglect to ask great things of our great God, for with Him, all things are possible.

11

Life Is Always in Forward Motion

You hem me in, behind and before, and lay your hand upon me. Such knowledge is too wonderful for me; it is high; I cannot attain it.

Psalm 139:5–6, ESV

LIVING IN forward motion is one of life's hard things. Right? We understand that Scripture tells us that God is with us. But often the unknown future seems overwhelming and a little scary—or sometimes a *lot* scary. Why? Because even though we intellectually know and believe that God will be with us, we don't experientially believe it. Here is the rub.

As Christians we can say we believe God's truth about everything from creation in seven literal days to Jesus' bodily resurrection in three literal days. We believe these to be true because God's Word tells us it is so. But when it comes to having the faith to face our uncertain tomorrows with courage, we frequently quake inside from the fear of it.

How does this disjoint in belief even make sense? For if we worship the God who created the earth in seven days and raised

Jesus from the dead, surely we can trust Him to oversee the length of our days, right?

We are being honest when we proclaim that we believe the truths found throughout Scripture and have no doubts that God did, and does, perform miracles and supernatural happenings that coincide perfectly with His written Word. In this way, we are full-of-faith believers who never doubt God and His Word.

However, when it comes to believing Him for our future well-being, we take exception. Shame on us. For when we fail to take God at His word, we disparage Him. We are, in fact, saying He is not trustworthy, and He is not able to care for His own.

We know that life is always moving in forward motion; there is no going back or making time stand still, so we must reckon with the scary truth that tomorrow is, and always will be, an incalculable unknown to our human minds. We cannot understand or predict our future in any certainty, other than to know we are sealed for all eternity in Christ. Life is in itself an unknown variable that is constantly a moving, changing, and untamable entity.

Therefore, we must develop a rock solid belief that God is good, God is faithful, God is sovereign, and God only wants what is best for us. Even when we claim to know this in an intellectual manner, we must go deeper and know, really know, these truths in the deepest parts of our soul. We must *know* that we know God will walk behind and before us, and He will lay His hand upon us, signifying His protection and His presence. God is with us. Always and forever.

As we mentally peruse the future with all its changing parts and shifting timelines, dare we neglect to solidify this basic Christian principle within our hearts and minds? No, we must not.

So today, when we are tempted to become overwhelmed by future what-ifs and unknowns, let us chart a very different course in a completely different direction. Instead of giving way to fearful thoughts and shaking knees, let us go back to what some people call the ACTS equation for prayer: Begin praying with Adoration. Follow with Confession. Next is Thanksgiving. End with Supplication.

Try this powerful prayer pattern both night and day for a week and see how big God grows in your estimation and how small your fear shrinks in direct relation. Grow forward in prayer so you can fearlessly live in forward motion.

My Heart's Cry

Father, the unknown future frightens me. I am often caught in an emotional downward spiral when I begin to contemplate all the what-ifs and the unknowns. Please help me to replace these harmful and paralyzing thoughts of unbelief with courage and faith. Give me the grace and strength I need to believe Your Word and to fully lean on Your goodness and abiding presence as I live my life in forward motion. The future may be hard but I know that You promise to be with me. Lord, let me never forget that You promise to hem me both behind and before and that Your hand will lay upon me. Amen.

We Can Do Hard Things

1. *Find hope and help in God's past provision.* Spend time alone with the Lord today, asking Him to help you remember accurately how present and protective He has been in your past. Focus on praising God for who He is and what He has done for you. Let your prayer be mainly adoration of our wondrous God, who always works for our good and displays His glory in the process.
2. *Find hope and help in God's present provision.* Today, as you pray, be sensitive to the areas in your life in which you need to confess your sins. Don't hold back by believing that any sin is a small matter beneath God's notice. Instead, invite God into

the conversation by admitting where you have faltered, and pray for renewal in your heart to allow His holy sanctifying process to continue in you every day.

3. *Find hope and help in God's future provision.* In your quiet time, pray with thanksgiving and supplication. Thank God for His goodness and His loving for care for you in the past, and ask Him to strengthen your faith for the future. Spend time asking God to shore up your heart when you feel overwhelmed and afraid of the unknowns. Then double back around to a time of thanksgiving, where true peace will flourish and grow. Determine to live in forward motion trusting in God all the way, every day.

12

Our Sanctification Is an Ongoing Process

And such were some of you. But you were washed, you were sanctified, you were justified in the name of the Lord Jesus Christ and by the Spirit of our God.
First Corinthians 6:11, ESV

SOME DAYS I JUST feel like I require a head-to-toe immersion from the Holy Spirit. Have you ever experienced one of those days when everything you attempted fell flat?

Maybe you attempted to bridge a communication roadblock, and instead the walls seemed to emerge stronger and more resistant than ever. You so hoped to have the opportunity to demonstrate a humble, contrite heart with an estranged loved one and the person was not interested in reconciling. Maybe you felt that old familiar resentment creep in from an old injury, and you gave way to the painful memories that left you feeling all hurt and rejected once again.

I believe we have all been in these oh-so-human spaces when, in our frailty and human weakness, we are simply not enough, and we know it. And contrary to our desires, this is exactly where God wants us.

He wants us to truly understand that each of us is a wretched sinner who needs saving and a lifetime of sanctifying. Yes, sanctifying is just another hard thing we have to accept, wrestle through, and keep moving through one day at a time. Sanctification is the process of being made pure and holy.

I experience the most discouragement when I pridefully believe I have conquered a specific sin and find out I haven't overcome it after all. In that uncomfortable and hard place, I have to ask for God's forgiveness—and maybe another's, depending upon the offense—then tuck in and start over . . . again and again.

Sometimes those "agains" feel like they reach toward eternity. I am tempted to give way to despair that I will ever conquer my sin this side of heaven.

But this is not the response God desires of me. He created each of us. He knows each of us is but dust and will return to dust. He knows each of our lives is but a wisp of wind and then we are no more.

He knows you. He knows me. Oh how thankful we should be that this is so, for it speaks volumes of God's great and magnificent love toward us all. The very Creator of the heavens and the earth has chosen to bestow His glorious and beneficent love on each of us.

So in those moments when we are tempted to despair over yet another sinful response, a hard-hearted attitude, a resentful posture, or a stubborn-minded stance, we must not give way to momentary discouragement that will surely paralyze us. Instead, we must choose to run to our gracious Father, beg for His mercy and forgiveness, thank Him for it, and move forward. Yes, we own up to our sin, we ask for pardon, and then we humbly step out to do our next thing.

Being such weaklings in faith and in life is hard, isn't it? And yet, knowing that God has designed us in this particular way, we must bow to His wisdom and His perfect plan and accept who we are.

And who we are is really quite astounding. We are God's own chosen ones. He calls us His beloved. He sets us as a seal upon His heart. Our names are written upon His hands. He is always only a prayer away—day and night. He goes before us and hems us in both behind and before. He is in our past, our present, and our future. He is God.

My Heart's Cry

Father, I have sinned against You and Your Word again. Countless times, I have failed, and I know I will fail again. Lord, help me to run swiftly to You when I sin. Give me the wisdom to never try to hide from You or to deny my sin, for You know it all already. Let this truth be a comfort to me. Help me to accept my human frailty. Help me to remember that You, God of the universe, designed me exactly as You saw best. Please strengthen my heart to not give in to discouragement but to humbly confess all to You and then thank You for Your great and gracious heart. I love You, Lord. Let the sanctification process You take me through bring You glory day by day. Amen.

We Can Do Hard Things

1. *Find hope and help in God's past provision.* Spend some time alone with God this week, recalling times when you felt as though you could never conquer your failings and faults. Spend some quiet moments in reflection, prayerfully asking God to illuminate those seasons when you felt especially discouraged over a specific, besetting sin. Then begin thanking Him for His gracious and ongoing forgiveness. Praise Him for the good work He is continuing in your life, for your good and His glory.

2. *Find hope and help in God's present provision.* As you contemplate the past week, ask the Lord to reveal to you any and all struggles you have experienced while fighting against sin. Ask God to show you your heart's true nature but don't stop there. Confess your sin to God and then thank Him for His faithful forgiveness and His steadfast love toward you. Ask Him to protect your heart against despair and discouragement in your day-to-day battle against sin. End with a time of rejoicing as you consider who you are and what you mean to our wondrous and magnificent God.
3. *Find hope and help in God's future provision.* Start with a time of confession before the Lord as you mentally look to the future. Ask Him to create in you a pure heart. Ask Him to help you focus on Him rather than all your past—and present—sinful failings. Then beseech God for His constant grace, strength, and hope, and ask for an eternal perspective on all things. Give thanks to God for creating you exactly as He desired—weaknesses and all—knowing that His glory and goodness shines all the brighter.

13

Learn from Others Who Have Gone Before Us

The memory of the righteous is a blessing, but the name of the wicked will rot.

Proverbs 10:7, ESV

I HAVE A FRIEND who is a history buff. She can name just about any date, time, and place that you quiz her on. She knows her stuff.

Sometimes, I feel envious of such a magnificent memory. My friend's ability to call up such details when asked offers another bonus—she can tell you what was happening all around these key junctures in history, as well. Whether it was a battle of immense proportions or a tiny victory in a remote seaside village, my friend can provide a colorful picture that includes all the important facts of that period.

Why does this type of memory impress me? Well, I would like to believe I can do the same when it comes to perfect recall of biblical events throughout history. Those are the need-to-know kind of stories we must have if we don't want to repeat others' mistakes. Right?

We use one of the most effective tools in our spiritual toolbox when we decide to remember. God told the Israelites to remember, remember, and remember. But did they? Do we?

Not so much. When we take the time to revisit the many mishaps that surrounded the journey from slavery to freedom, we can't help but notice how often the Israelites got into hot water for one simple reason: they forgot. They failed to obey God's command to become good rememberers of what God had done for them.

To be clear, at times calling to mind their past incidences of disobedience and sinfulness was hard to do. And it is difficult when God calls us to do the same.

And yet, God has never wavered on this single admonition to His people from all centuries: Remember, remember, remember.

When we obey God and take those much-needed hard looks at our own failures, God teaches us good life lessons. Hard lessons to be sure—but life-giving lessons.

As Proverbs 10 tells us, the memory of the righteous is a blessing, and don't we each want to be remembered as one of God's righteous ones? What we choose to do today, and choose to remember, will, in great part, determine our legacy for Christ. For each of us has a list of failings and frailties that expose our bent toward sinfulness and self-will.

We are given the Bible, in part, to help us remember and to help us avoid the sins of those who have gone before us. Their choices—both the good and the bad—will help equip us in our battle against sin.

But we must take heed. We must be willing to take long, hard looks at our own hearts. We must be willing to confess and forsake every one of our sins. We must learn to discipline ourselves to the study of Scripture, where God can continually shine the light of His perfect truth upon our hearts.

So today, ask God to give you a mind that is willing to remember both the good and the hard things from your past so you will better avoid those same sins in the coming days.

My Heart's Cry

Father, please help me to grow into a good rememberer. I understand that those who have gone before me can teach me important life lessons. I want to remember so that I do not sin against You. But I also know I can find much wisdom in paying attention to those who have gone before me. It is hard, I admit, to think about my own past sin and failings. But I must do so at times so that I recall the painful repercussions of my own waywardness of heart. Help me, Lord, to take heed to the lessons You have revealed throughout Scripture and to walk wisely all the days of my life. Amen.

We Can Do Hard Things

1. *Find hope and help in God's past provision.* As you spend time today with the Lord, choose to remember—and remember well. Ask God to reveal to your mind those moments, good or hard, when you did or did not obey. Pray that God will help you to use the past as a springboard to learn from your mistakes and to avoid the same sins in the future. Thank Him for His ability to transform even your worst failings into something He can use for good.
2. *Find hope and help in God's present provision.* Today, ask God to help you pinpoint specific Bible characters from both the Old and New Testament you can identify with most. Reread your favorite stories of their failures and successes. Then write any similarities between your current struggles and those they faced in the past. Learn from them and give thanks to God for these vital life lessons that are eternal in scope.
3. *Find hope and help in God's future provision.* Take some quiet moments to reflect upon your past and present challenges. Then ask God to help you to glean fresh insights and wisdom for the future. Pray that God will create in you a sensitive

spirit and a willing heart to make a change of direction, when necessary, in the coming weeks and months. Look to the future with hope and encouragement because you understand that our heavenly Father is faithful to bring transformation from even our darkest and deepest sins. For our good and His glory, God always has the final say in the history of the world and in each of our lives.

14

Develop a Humble, Dependent Heart

I keep my eyes always on the Lord. With him at my right hand, I will not be shaken.

Psalm 16:8

WHEN A CLOSE friend got a distressing telephone call from her sister's medical team, she literally collapsed onto the floor. Just the day before she had received the surprising but welcome news that her older sister was being taken out of hospice care because she was improving. She rejoiced in that wonderful news. Less than twenty-four hours later, however, her sister had died. How to process this roller coaster of emotions?

My friend could not even express what she was feeling because a numbness permeated her entire being. After the initial shock, she got up and began calling family and friends. Each time she spoke with another family member, she had to relive the distressing news, so she shut down emotionally.

Some might call it the body's instinctive way of protecting itself when we are called upon to deal with the harsh realities of life. Others might attribute such a numbness to God's way of helping us cope with tragedy.

However we choose to view our emotional responses in the face of hard news, the reality is the same. God has to take over, and we totally depend on Him for what we cannot be or say or do in light of such personal heartache and sorrow.

My friend realized this truth in the hours and days after her sister's passing. She didn't have to experience emotions of any kind to know a deeper, more powerful truth: God was at her right hand, and because of that precious promise, she would not be shaken. As my dear friend processed her sister's sudden death, she learned that the more she consciously depended on the Lord, the better.

She prayed constantly that God would give her a humble heart and a dependent posture as she coped with planning the funeral, cleaning out her sister's home, and acting as executor of her estate. Many moments during those emotionally volatile days following her sister's death, my friend recognized that the more she turned her grieving gaze toward the Lord, the calmer and more peaceful she felt.

Saying goodbye to our loved ones and friends is one of life's hardest challenges. It can break us and send us headlong into despair if we allow it to do so. But as believers, we don't have to sorrow as the world sorrows, because we have hope. We have hope beyond measure for we know we will be reunited with our loved ones in heaven if they were believers, too.

As the weeks and months passed, my friend learned so much about herself and what she valued above all else. She learned we must put our highest priority on obeying Jesus' final command to go and tell; make disciples.

This is our calling and our life's greatest work. When someone we love passes into eternity, it gives us opportunity for lots of introspection. This is a good, albeit hard, thing. We need to reflect upon our own lives and how carefully we heed Christ's admonition.

Many of us have already shared the gospel with our loved ones, and they have rejected it. As we grieve, God still calls us to do hard things, and sharing the gospel is one of them.

When we suffer any type of loss, it hurts. But for the believer, the sting of death has been removed. Thank God. We can become a lighthouse of sorts to those around us who are grieving bitterly over their losses. God gives us the truth to share, the words to speak, and the love to extend. Let's pray that when we next have to face the searing pain of death, we immediately run to Jesus in humility and dependence so we can become fit vessels to share His gospel with everyone who has ears to hear.

My Heart's Cry

Father, today I felt shaken to my core when I learned of my loved one's death. I was so surprised by this. And then my emotions suddenly went from a heightened extreme to an eerie numbness. That was frightening. I couldn't even feel the emotions I thought I should feel. Thank You, Lord, for helping me to keep my gaze fixed upon You. As soon as I looked to You, I felt safe and secure. Help me, Father, to have the courage and the words to share Your love with others who are mourning without hope. Give me the opportunity to tell of Your sacrifice on the cross. Let my mind be fixed on You, and let my heart be fixed on sharing the good news. Amen.

We Can Do Hard Things

1. *Find hope and help in God's past provision.* During time alone with God, ask Him to remind you of past losses when your emotions threatened to control you. Ask God to bring to your mind how He met you in your time of sorrow and covered you with His perfect love and protection. Thank Him for His sheltering care, even when your heart was breaking.

2. *Find hope and help in God's present provision.* Today, as you seek the Lord, ask Him to give you the wisdom and strength to keep your eyes fixed upon Him. Ask God to protect you from needless worries and temporary burdens as you journey through a season of loss. Thank Him that because He has promised to be at your right hand, you never need be shaken.
3. *Find hope and help in God's future provision.* As you process your grief, thank the Lord that He wants you to completely depend upon Him. Give Him thanks that His desire for you to keep your gaze upon Him will help you work through your sorrow. Pray for a willing and humble heart that finds comfort in God alone. Then ask God to give you opportunities to share His good news with those who are mourning without hope.

15

Learn to Lean On God More Completely

The LORD will fight for you,
and you have only to be silent.

Exodus 14:14, ESV

AN ACQUAINTANCE of mine has been counseling a young mother of four boys who is in the midst of a contentious divorce she did not want. This mother did all she could to save her marriage. She sought biblical counseling faithfully each week. She worked with the pastor and elders of her church to try to salvage this marriage. She spent hours upon her knees asking God to perform a miracle and bring her estranged husband back home.

All this effort and commitment and love seemed to be for nothing, at least from her human perspective. And just when those who love her and her boys believed it couldn't get any worse another bombshell dropped. Her most recent challenge in this endless season of heartache is the damaging way her spouse is treating their children. This wayward father verbally abuses the boys each time he is with them and makes them feel it's their fault the marriage foundered.

She felt agonized enough when the battle was between her and her spouse. But now that the father has begun making the children pawns in the divorce, the pain is beyond imaginable. She hurts in a way she never dreamed possible.

This dedicated and stalwart mom is doing all she can to protect her boys and soothe their emotions after interactions with their father. But some hurts reach the deepest part of a person's heart and soul, where no human can heal them. So my friend has, in a sense, given the care of her precious sons into God's hands. She knows God is powerful enough to secure their safety. How right she is.

When we face battles beyond our strength, God is truly the one who fights for us. As this passage in Exodus reminds us, "The LORD will fight for you, and you have only to be silent."

What a precious and impactful statement! The Lord God Himself will fight our battles. Our part? We have only to be silent.

Perhaps one enlightening portion of this mighty promise from our heavenly Father is that our words frequently get us mired more deeply in conflicts with others. Our emotions can take over, and we begin to react instead of acting.

A huge difference lies between these two choices. When we react, we allow another's words and sins against us to result in our lashing out or retaliating. However, when we stand back, keep our silence, trust our God, we are choosing to act—as one who knows the Lord and is living as an image bearer of Him.

Once the verbal sparring matches began between her husband and their boys, this faith-full mom learned to pray that God would fight for her and them. And she learned to be silent, speaking only when necessary and productive.

All who witnessed the potentially volatile hard interactions realized that her spouse wanted a fight. When she refused to enter the verbal fray, her husband's anger didn't dissipate, but hers did.

So one hard conversation at a time, this dear, believing mom has chosen to lean on God completely, and He hasn't let her down. Certainly, this is a hard season, but she has hope because she knows her heavenly Father will fight for her, and she need only be silent.

My Heart's Cry

Father, I am in a situation that is breaking my heart in so many pieces I wonder if I will make it through the day. Help me, please. Come close to me and let me know the comfort of Your loving and powerful presence. Don't let me give up hope. My family depends on me to keep the faith and stay calm amid all this upheaval. I never, ever wanted to be in this situation. But I am here, not by my own choice. You know this, Lord. You know my heart. Please give me what I need just for today, and help me to not mentally step into tomorrow. I am Yours, and I am so grateful to call You my Father. Amen.

We Can Do Hard Things

1. *Find hope and help in God's past provision.* When you feel overwhelmed by today's hard things in your life, think back to past difficult seasons. Choose to focus upon God's faithfulness to you during those hard times. Choose to remember the significant ways that God reached down and touched your life to embolden and encourage you. Then give thanks that you serve that same faithful God today.
2. *Find hope and help in God's present provision.* Begin writing a list of ways that God is currently meeting you in your hardship and pain. Document every blessing and ounce of goodness you can identify. Once you have a list compiled, linger over each item on it. Consider how lovingly and tenderly God has orchestrated these personal blessings tailored just for

you. Then give Him thanks. Give the God of the universe—your God—the praise and worship He deserves.

3. *Find hope and help in God's future provision.* Focus on doing your part as you contemplate your unknown tomorrows with the knowledge that God has promised to fight for you. Meditate upon this passage from Exodus and think about what it means for you today and through all your tomorrows. Come what may, God has promised to fight for you. You need only be silent. Take time to sit in silence before God today and think only of Him and who He is for you.

16

Understand that Grace Is Given When We Obey

But if you carefully obey his voice and do all that I say, then I will be an enemy to your enemies and an adversary to your adversaries.

Exodus 23:22, ESV

SOMETIMES WE ARE our own enemies. Sometimes we create the messes in which we are currently mired. Sometimes simple disobedience lands us in hard times. Then we wonder where God is as we suffer. Wretched sinners that we all are, this truth should be both a warning and a reminder to us that obedience matters. God tells us to read His Word and to obey its commands. He expects nothing less from us as His beloved children.

Still, how often do we run to the Lord and cry out to Him in our pain, asking Him to deliver us from it without a second thought as to how we got into this present hard situation? This is indeed a painful truth. I fear that often we are like the child who cries because he or she got caught doing something wrong rather than repenting because we have disobeyed and offended our God.

But we must learn the value of obedience in every area of our lives. As we walk in obedience to God's commands, we will certainly falter and fall. God knows this about us. God graciously forgives us of our sins. But the rub is that He doesn't promise us grace in the midst of our sinful acts and rebellion against His mandates.

When we deliberately walk our way—away from the Lord—and disregard God's commands and warnings, we can expect to suffer painful and uncomfortable consequences. However, we cannot expect God's grace to flow down from the heavens as we persistently continue in our sin.

God's grace is a wondrous gift, available to us always. But God loves us too much to allow us to continue in our waywardness. He will often draw us back to Him by allowing our suffering and sorrow to multiply until we turn back to Him.

Yes, we will all endure hard times and have to do hard things. But let's not, by our own disobedience, make living in this broken, sin-ridden world even more difficult than it already is.

It matters to God that we follow His Word and remember that Jesus told His disciples that they prove their love for Him by simply obeying Him. Straightforward and simply stated, Jesus said, "If you love me, you will follow my commands."

Yet, even in the face of such a clear exhortation, many will falsely contend that because of God's grace, everything is permissible—even blatant sin. This could not be further from the truth or the intent of Scripture.

God gives us grace to obey Him—not as an excuse to pursue worldly lusts, but He gives us the power to resist sin. As this passage in Exodus states, when we carefully obey His voice and do all He says, then He will become an enemy to our enemies and an adversary to our adversaries.

Who among us doesn't want to experience this promise? The very God of the universe promises to protect us and shelter us from our enemies. So today, when we are tempted to minimize our sin, let's not forget what God has commanded, for we all need His grace and strength every hour to battle against life's hard things.

My Heart's Cry

Father, please forgive me for not battling harder against my sinfulness. I tend to minimize my sin and to make excuses for it. Help me to view my sin first as an offense against You, Lord. Then let me swiftly ask for Your forgiveness before making amends as needed. I am so tempted to compare my failings with others so I can feel better about myself. Lord, You call this foolishness when we compare ourselves to one another. Instead, I must compare myself to Jesus and the high standard of holiness He set before us all. Please forgive me for my stubborn and willful heart. Cleanse me from all unrighteousness, and create in me a willing spirit. Amen.

We Can Do Hard Things

1. *Find hope and help in God's past provision.* When you arise this week, spend time thanking God for His goodness and grace, as you remember those moments when you sinned and strayed from Him. Praise God for His persistent love toward you that wouldn't allow you to stay mired in your sin. Remember and learn from your mistakes so that you don't stray down that wayward path again.
2. *Find hope and help in God's present provision.* As you prepare for today's tasks, ask God to cleanse you from all unrighteousness and to create in you a willing spirit. Pray that God will give you the desire to obey Him even when it hurts, even when it means great personal sacrifice. Then, prayerfully beseech God to open your eyes to any areas of your life in which you are sinning, and ask for the grace to battle against it.
3. *Find hope and help in God's future provision.* At bedtime this week, spend quiet moments reflecting on your past and current struggles against sin. Look for patterns and circumstances that tempt you to make excuses for your sin.

Then ask the Lord to create in you a sensitive spirit that identifies these potential dangers so you can run from them. Pray that God will remind you of the seriousness of willing disobedience. Remember how His grace is given to those who actively pursue and live in obedience to Him. Pray for a desire to obey God, as evidence that you love Him above all other things.

17

Stop Defining Failure as a Bad Thing

In all their distress he too was distressed, and the angel of his presence saved them. In his love and mercy he redeemed them; he lifted them up and carried them all the days of old.

Isaiah 63:9

FAILURE IS A many-faceted entity that every human is closely familiar with, because we all fail. We all sin. We are all in need of a Savior and a Sustainer every moment of every day of our lives. This is why I am surprised when I become overwrought and disheartened by my own failure. *When will I learn,* I ask myself? *When will I finally conquer this besetting sin? When will I stop myself before saying something I will regret?*

Do you know the feeling? We all have specific areas of weakness where we can be especially tempted to falter and fall into sin. I know it and you know it. Since we are all unique with different backgrounds and home lives, my story will be unlike yours.

But God wants so much more for us than for us to continually walk in despair and defeat when we fail. From God's divine perspective, this is the perfect training arena for future success.

Think about it. When we fail we are at our lowest point emotionally, mentally, and often physically. Failure can make us literally ill. And when we are at our lowest plain, this is when God, in a mighty, loving gesture reaches down to us and draws us in.

Yes, failure is a hard thing to stomach, but it can also be the making of us as God uses each failure to mold us into the image of His beloved Son, Jesus.

In this passage of Isaiah, we read how God is distressed when we are distressed. In His love and mercy, He redeems us and then He lifts us up and carries us as He did in days of old. God is distressed for us because we are hurting, and He is our healer.

Reread that truth again and again until it takes root in the deepest part of your soul. God is distressed when we are distressed.

What a God we serve! None of us deserves to be adopted into the family of God. None of us deserves constant and continual forgiveness—but God grants it as we ask for His pardon and His restoration. None of us can claim to be without failure, without some residue of sin hidden within our hearts, and yet our mighty God loves us so much that He is distressed when we are distressed.

So when you next experience that feeling of shame and regret over yet another failure, another sin, run headlong to Jesus' open arms. Run to Him alone.

Beg His forgiveness and receive it. Then know—really know—that no matter what you have done, no matter how many times you have failed, He is there to open wide His heart to you, His beloved child.

Know this: In all our distress, our God is distressed. He hurts right along with us, and He is distressed that we are distressed. This is the loving, forgiving, all-powerful God we love and serve.

Let Him, in His magnificent love and mercy, redeem you, lift you up, and carry you as He did for His people in the past. Let God minister to you in your failure and rejoice in you when you get it right. Our God never alters or changes. He is not fickle with emotions as are we. He is always the same—today, tomorrow, and forever. Bless His name.

My Heart's Cry

Father, here I am again asking for Your forgiveness and pardon. I feel so discouraged, so beaten down. I want to give up. How many more times will I run back to You, pleading for Your forgiveness for the same sin? I cannot even think about it without feeling shame and remorse. But I know You do forgive me. I know You want me to come running back to You when I falter. You desire an intimate relationship with me because You created me. You chose me to be part of Your family. Thank You, Lord. I am overcome by the thought that You are distressed when I am distressed. It is beyond my understanding that the perfect God of the universe commiserates with me in my failings. Please help me to not lose hope, to not lose heart, but to keep running back to You for forgiveness and the restoration I so desperately need. Amen.

We Can Do Hard Things

1. *Find hope and help in God's past provision.* Prayerfully bring to mind those areas of your life when you sinned in ways that left you feeling distressed and despairing that you would ever find victory. Then ask God to show you how He was working in you during those times. Ask Him to reveal to you how you have matured through your failure. Then thank Him for being with you in the battle. Thank Him for caring so much that He, too, was distressed when you were distressed. Praise God for His incomprehensible love.
2. *Find hope and help in God's present provision.* Today if you are mired in the feelings of discouragement or feeling overwhelmed by your inability to conquer a besetting sin, run to God. Let

Him cover you with His forgiveness, which He grants freely and unendingly. Sit with God in silence and let His Holy Spirit fill you again, comfort you, and teach you. Then give Him thanks for His perfect love that never, ever gives up on you.

3. *Find hope and help in God's future provision.* Take time to be alone with God this week, to contemplate how you believe God is nudging you to grow. Even in the hard things, the hard setbacks, the hard changes, God will make a way, sustain, and strengthen you as you seek to grow in sanctification. Thank Him for the mercy He bestows on you every day and how He only wants the very best for you. Then praise Him for who He is and how limitless He is to bring about these transformations in your life.

18

When God Is Big

I am the Lord, the God of all mankind.
Is anything too hard for me?

Jeremiah 32:27

WHEN MY YOUNGEST daughter was admitted to the hospital for the birth of her firstborn, I was elated. She had endured one of the most difficult pregnancies I had ever been aware of. My daughter suffers from severe scoliosis, and this malady triggered unimaginable pain and complex physical hurdles. She also had fibroids, which further complicated her pregnancy—and yes, caused immense and constant pain.

After one trip to the emergency room, she was admitted to the hospital for five days, and other issues came to light. It was as though one condition triggered another—a sad and dismal domino effect took place before our eyes and broke our hearts.

As her mom, I cried. And I cried out to the Lord continually. I asked Him to heal her body, to spare her from more suffering, and to bring such a turnaround of events that everyone would know that He healed her and that God would get the glory.

But that didn't happen. Instead, God, in His divine wisdom and sovereignty, gave my daughter daily grace and strength to endure her suffering rather than heal her. Many nights, I prayed to the Lord that He would have mercy on my dear child and end this long, extremely hard season. But His answer was no.

To be truthful, I had a hard time with God's plan for my daughter. As a mother, I would do anything to stop my children from enduring such physical pain. But even as I write these words I know weightier considerations exist than the alleviation of physical pain. God has a much bigger, much grander plan than I can ever conceive of.

So I must trust Him. Without question. Without debate. Without hesitation. I must bow before His sovereign will in every circumstance and, like it or not, continue to trust and obey.

During some of my daughter's more agonizing moments, I dropped to my knees and prayed for God's hand of comfort and care to descend upon my child in a way she would recognize. I beseeched the God of heavens and earth to make Himself known to her, so she would have endurance and hope.

And you know what? He did that. I didn't always hear of these intimate accounts right away, but at the right time, my daughter would share with me how God had met her in her time of hardship and desperation for relief. Again, I dropped to my knees and prayed—with a heart full of thanksgiving and praise.

God grew bigger to me in those moments. Did He alter or change? No. But my realization of His greatness was enlarged exponentially.

God allowed me, as a bystander to my child's pain, to witness how He would uphold her, love her, sustain her, and change her. Yes, God is always in the business of making the most of our pain. As Elizabeth Elliot was so fond of saying, "Suffering is never for nothing."

She was correct. God uses our pain, whether large or small, to remind us of our complete dependence upon Him. And He often parts the curtains so we can witness what He is doing of eternal import.

Amid all of our hard things, God is at the very center. He is there, with us—strengthening, sustaining, and loving us as our beloved Father.

As for my daughter, she gave birth to a beautiful baby boy. Her pain didn't end when she entered the hospital. It was a long and harrowing delivery, and at one point, they feared they had lost their precious baby. But God intervened. He in His mercy and love breathed life into our newest grandson.

Yes, life is so full of hard things—difficult seasons and painful losses. And still, we can turn to God again and again and again in full confidence that He hears us. Our God listens to His children's prayers. He is our great and mighty and big God. Praise Him.

My Heart's Cry

Father, I feel completely undone. I have no strength. I don't even have any more words to offer in prayer. I feel spent both in body and in spirit. Again, I wonder, how long, Lord? How long will this season of suffering last, and do I have the strength to endure it? Please help me, Lord. Come close to me so that I sense Your Spirit and find comfort in Your protection and care. Help me to keep my eyes fixed on You and not on these hard circumstances. And strengthen my faith so I do not quit interceding for my loved ones. Help me, Father, to see Your grandness and glory and to never forget how big You are. Amen.

We Can Do Hard Things

1. *Find hope and help in God's past provision.* Take all the time you need to sit in silence before the Lord to recall in detail moments when God met you in your time of great need. Remember first those circumstances that left you feeling small and bereft of hope. Then choose to remember how God stepped onto the scene and met your needs in miraculous ways. Thank Him for His goodness and His greatness.

2. *Find hope and help in God's present provision.* Today spend time in prayer, asking God to help you reframe your present struggles, trials, and difficulties. Ask God to give you eyes to see the grand work of transformation and redemption He is actively doing on your behalf. Pray that God gives you the eyes of faith to see how big He truly is—and how small our temporal suffering is in light of eternity. Find joy in God's future faithfulness. As you contemplate days ahead, do not take on tomorrow's worries. As you fight for joy today, remember that God is in the midst of your present suffering and transforming your heart and mind. Thank Him that He is teaching you what it means to face hard things and to suffer well as you trust Him completely.
3. *Find hope and help in God's future provision.* As you contemplate the unknown and often-hard and scary future, ask the Lord to redirect your heart and mind to Him. Ask the Lord to remind you of specific verses and promises of truth to shore up your weak and needy soul. Pray every day for God to open your spiritual eyes so you can see the eternal good God is doing in you and around you and through you. Amen.

19

Fear God, Not People

The fear of man lays a snare,
but whoever trusts in the LORD is safe.

Proverbs 29:25, ESV

SOMETIMES GOD calls us to say "yes" and do hard things for Him. At other times, God calls us to say "no," and it's hard. Huh? Indeed, many times we don't feel up to saying "yes" when asked to serve, to get involved, and to make a difference, but we are afraid to decline. Why is this?

Simple. We all suffer from the fear of humans and it's a sinful posture to adopt. God wants us to be free of this fickle and slavish mentality. God wants us to fear Him alone.

As we learn to put God in His proper place—as God of the universe and Creator of heaven and earth—He sets us free from our people-pleasing mentality. As this verse in Proverbs states, the fear of man lays a snare, but when we trust in the Lord we are safe.

Let's look at a real world example of what an appropriate "no" looks like. Consider that you are caring for your teenage children and your elderly father and are serving as the children's director at your church. Then an acquaintance invites you to a fundraising banquet, where you are asked to volunteer two evenings a week in a group home for single mothers.

Your heart knows the value of this ministry to unwed mothers. Your heart goes out to their terrible plight and you love babies! So what's the hesitation?

This is the juncture where we must be willing to say "no" and to be willing to disappoint, or even anger, another person who doesn't understand our already heavy load. When we fear people rather than God, we enslave ourselves to the whims and wishes of anyone who requests our help—well-intentioned or not.

Each of us is limited in strength and energy, limited in time and resources, limited in every capacity—and we must acknowledge it. So instead of falling into the false guilt trap, we need to be as prayerful about saying "yes" as we are about saying "no." For only God knows the path He has designated for us during any specific season.

Is it hard to say no? Yes, indeed. It can be especially difficult to decline a request when we recognize the value of whatever organization or ministry opportunity approaches us to get involved. And still, God reminds us that fear of humans—and their response to us—lays a snare every time.

We are only beholden to God. We must learn to say the hard "no" when it is the wisest choice for our lives, given our current commitments. God would rather we listen closely and heed His guidance to do only what He has called us to do and do it well. Rather than heedlessly or impulsively saying "yes" whenever we are asked to serve, we must learn to stop ourselves from a hasty "yes," which we will regret.

Again, sometimes saying "yes" can be hard. But I wonder if it isn't more difficult to learn to say "no." It has been for me. When we truly desire to obey our Lord, serving others is non-negotiable. However, all service, at all seasons of life, must be put through the grid of prayer, wise counsel, and time to thoughtfully consider.

So today if you are being pressured to take on yet another serving responsibility, and you are barely surviving your current obligations, pause and pray. Ask God to give you the wisdom to say "no" if needed and the courage to do the hard thing—and not worry about how people will view you if you decline. Fear God alone, and be free.

My Heart's Cry

Father, please give me Your wisdom to know when to say "yes" and when to say "no." I find it difficult to say "no" to someone when they ask me to serve. You know my heart desires to love and serve the needs of those around me. I try to be faithful to being sensitive and open to whomever and wherever You call me to make a difference. But at this season of my life, I already feel stretched thin by my family and church obligations. You know how often I ask You for the grace and strength to continue. Please set me free from the fear of humans, for I recognize it is a snare. Help me to fear You alone and to be set free from the inside out. Amen.

We Can Do Hard Things

1. *Find hope and help in God's past provision.* Remember all the ways God provided for you in past seasons when you felt overwhelmed by the tasks you were committed to fulfilling. Thank Him for how He met you every day in your space of service and provided the energy and stamina to see your responsibilities through. Then reflect on whether or not you were overcommitted. Were you attentive to God's leading? Or did you overcommit because you were afraid of someone's rejection or anger if you said no.
2. *Find hope and help in God's present provision.* As you begin your day, spend some moments asking the Lord to give you His divine wisdom and understanding as it pertains to saying "yes" and saying "no." Ask God to give you a discerning heart

that is courageous enough to say a hard "no" when appropriate. Finally, ask Him to help you fear only Him and to rid yourself of the fear of people.

3. *Find hope and help in God's future provision.* As you plan for future months, ask God for wisdom, understanding, insight, and courage. Ask Him to open your eyes to areas of opportunity in which He wants you to become involved. Then ask God to give you the strength to say "no" even when it's hard. Pray for a heart that seeks only to please Him.

20

Faithful Overcomers in Scripture

For everyone who has been born of God overcomes the world. And this is the victory that has overcome the world—our faith.

First John 5:4, ESV

WE TRULY MISS one of life's greatest teaching opportunities when we fail to dig deeply into both the Old and New Testaments for examples of men and women of the faith who can only be described as overcomers.

God, in His mercy and kindness, allows us the insider's view to the foibles and failings of many believers throughout the ages. He could have ordained the Bible to only contain history's success stories but He didn't. God in His gracious generosity of Spirit allows us to get to know about the men and women of faith who came before us.

What a tremendous gift this is for every believer in today's world. We can open the Word and find one example after another of people who lived for the Lord and, like us, sometimes faltered or failed. Life was as hard for them as it is hard for us. These men and women from years past were of the same physical, mental, emotional, and spiritual makeup as we are today.

So, as we take the time to dig into their lives and seek to understand their challenges and difficulties, we, too, can take heart and learn from them and their mistakes. God offers us information so we can fully appreciate how challenging their lives were from social, economic, political, and religious terms.

Like us, they had to battle a world that was antagonistic against the purity and truth of God's directives. Like us, they had to wage war against unbelieving counterparts who opposed living a holy life of faith. And, like us, they understood the price they would need to pay for their faithfulness to God.

I wonder how many of us have taken the time and energy to research the biblical individuals who gave their very lives for their belief in God and faith in Jesus. The deeper I delve into the rich scriptures about these men and women of faith, the more I see reflections of my own life.

I identify with their struggles to maintain a vibrant, active faith in a world so opposed to everything held as sacred. I understand how they grew discouraged and even despondent after fighting evil in its many unrelenting forms. I relate to their waves of fear and lack of courage. In truth, I see myself in every single example of weakness I read about—and I cry out to God to help me.

Reading the Bible is not for the faint of heart. Some stories shake us to the core or convict us. It can be hard when you recognize yourself—and your sin and weaknesses—in the pages of biblical characters' stories.

And yet isn't that the response God desires of us? He wants us to understand although we may live in today's tech-savvy world, our internal fight is the same as theirs. He tells us all about their lives—the good, the bad, and the ugly—so we glean from their errors and learn to walk a different way.

Thank God for these men and women who, through the sovereign will of God, reveal to us what it means to walk rightly and what the repercussions are when we choose to disobey.

Today, when you begin to feel that no one understands the hardships you face, go to Scripture. Research the lives of men and women of the Bible and learn about them. Learn from them and be blessed.

My Heart's Cry

Father, help me today to better understand that I am no different than the men and women found throughout Scripture. Thank You for ordaining that they be represented in all their humanity and frailty. This encourages me. I would not be able to relate to perfect examples of faith because I know how flawed I am. Please help me to understand how valuable their stories are to my own walk with You. Guide me as I search their stories, and help me glean eternal truths from studying their lives. And never let me forget that their lives were just as hard as mine is today. Thank You for giving us such a rich resource from which to grow and learn and be encouraged. Amen.

We Can Do Hard Things

1. *Find hope and help in God's past provision.* Spend time this week researching at least one biblical character from the Old Testament and one from the New Testament. Use any notes in your Bible, along with a commentary and even listen to others' messages on the men or women you study. Note the person's strengths and weaknesses, as well as his or her challenges. Observe how God worked within the people you chose to strengthen and grow them in their faith.
2. *Find hope and help in God's present provision.* As you go through the week, ask God to bring to your mind biblical

characters who have always stood out to you because of their responses to hard times. Think of Noah, Moses, Joseph, Esther, Mary, Paul, and others. Then choose one of these men or women and study his or her life. Journal about any similarities between yourself and the person. Ask God to help you fully understand how He used his or her hard times to sanctify and mature the person.

3. *Find hope and help in God's future provision.* As you consider the future, remember men and women from Scripture who faced the unknown future and recognized how they each handled their fears and worries. Review their stories and write their responses. Note how God met each one in his or her time of need and how He encouraged and strengthened these people when they felt lost and anxious. Study how God used their times of trepidation and fear to embolden and develop their faith.

21

Take a Deep Dive into the Proverbs

Blessed is the one who finds wisdom, and the one who gets understanding, for the gain from her is better than gain from silver and her profit better than gold. She is more precious than jewels, and nothing you can desire can compare with her.

Proverbs 3:13–15, ESV

LONG AGO, a godly friend gave me a recommended Bible study program, which included reading a chapter from the book of Proverbs that corresponded with each day of the month. Every day, every month, I read that day's proverb.

I have to say that has been one of the wisest decisions I've ever made. When we choose to spend time pouring over the book in the Bible that is known for its wisdom-imparting principles, we are the gainers.

In the same way, all those near and dear to us are beneficiaries, too. How so? If we read and act upon the creeds and principles found in Proverbs, our attitudes, our thoughts, our choices, our words, and our actions will reflect these biblical precepts. Who wouldn't want to pal around folks who are wise?

In our sin-ridden world, it only makes sense that believers take full advantage of the precious jewels and better-than-silver-or-gold precepts God has bestowed upon us. But do we? I fear that many Christians are not as invested in this treasure trove found in God's Word as they should be.

Each of us must determine the pattern in which we seek to know and learn from God. We must pick and choose between our Bible and other ways of learning about God. Of late, I've noticed a trend that is gaining precedence: a growing neglect of reading the Bible in favor of listening to podcasts and reading books—even worthy Christian books. This should not be.

Our foremost priority should be to immerse ourselves in God's Word. Secondly, we have to determine what add-ons to include in our daily time with the Lord. This frequently flipped upside down when believers place more emphasis on what their favorite Bible teacher communicates than on what God's Word says to us. So we must take a good, hard look at the content that fills our quiet time with God.

First, ask yourself if you are following a yearly Bible reading plan. If not, find one and stick to it. Then ask yourself how deeply you delve into whatever book in the Bible you are currently reading.

Do you take enough time to read the text and absorb its meaning—and then, also read any notes pertaining to these verses? Do you ever cross-reference verses that jump out at you? Do you copy specific verses into your journal or cards to meditate upon during the day?

These are just a few simple ways to glean more out of the text of the Bible. They are especially helpful in the book of Proverbs, which is known for its wisdom for living a godly life.

Each day, we have to make hard choices regarding how we spend our limited time, energy, and resources. So it is of utmost importance that we invest time in God's Word, carefully ingesting

His truth—His powerful, living, and active Word that promises to transform us from the inside out.

As this passage from Proverbs tells us, we will be blessed when we find wisdom and understanding from reading (and meditating upon and obeying) the biblical principles in book of Proverbs. We will gain far more than silver, gold, or jewels.

And nothing that we desire can compare with the riches that are ours when we delve deeply into this life-altering and life-giving book. In this hard world, what better way than to equip ourselves to face our challenges than with the eternal wisdom and understanding we require and that stands against time and every foe under the sun?

My Heart's Cry

Father, I am in awe of the wisdom and understanding I gain from simply reading through Proverbs. Each day, I discover a fresh and new road map that helps me stay near to You and live in obedience to Your commands. Daily, I am amazed how the Holy Spirit brings these precepts to life for me. I often pray about how to face difficult challenges, and then I open Your Word, and my path becomes clear. Thank You, Lord, for giving me such an invaluable resource that will direct my comings and goings for my entire life. I don't have to doubt about what is a right or wrong decision when I have Your Words right before me. What a comfort this is to me and will continue to be throughout my life. Amen.

We Can Do Hard Things

1. *Find hope and help in God's past provision.* Spend time reading through Proverbs this week. Read several chapters each day, and highlight passages that stand out to you. As you read and reflect upon their wisdom-giving principles, ask the Lord to help you remember times past when you listened to and

obeyed these precious precepts and how God blessed your path because of your obedience.

2. *Find hope and help in God's present provision.* As you sit alone with God today, open your Bible to Proverbs and read the chapter that corresponds to today's date. Reread the whole chapter. Then highlight any verses that stand out to you, which will equip you to make decisions and act right now. Ask God to illuminate your understanding about any hard things you are facing by revealing any areas in which you need to change or redirect.
3. *Find hope and help in God future provision.* As you pray about the future, ask God to give you His divine wisdom and understanding. Ask Him to show you the way He wants you to take. Pray that God uses Proverbs to reveal any waywardness in your heart and mind. Thank Him for providing you with an infallible road map through life's sometimes confusing and unsettling roadways.

22

View Life through the Lens of Eternity

***He has made everything beautiful in its time.
Also, he has put eternity into man's heart.***

Ecclesiastes 3:11, ESV

WHEN TWO OF my daughters miscarried their unborn babies it changed them both. And it changed me. I remember getting emotionally devastating phone calls that shared their heartbreaking news. Between the two of them, they have suffered five miscarriages. Our family grieved together, and we each grieved privately.

I remember the day when a brand-new thought came to my mind after weeks of sorrow and grief. We would meet our dear grandbabies someday. In heaven, we would meet and be reunited forever. What a thought! What a promise! We have discussed this comforting reality many times through the years. Even today when people ask me how many grandchildren we have, I almost always say, "We are blessed with seven here on earth and five more in heaven." I never, ever want to forget God's promises of this.

Remembering that we will meet our grandbabies in the eternal heaven does more than comfort me because of our loss. It shores me up for the hard things I have to face today. It reminds me that I serve the God of the past, present, and future. It brings to my mind how magnificent God is and how He created these little ones before the foundation of the world. He knew their frame before time began, says Psalm 139.

This act of recalling God's mighty promises and resurrection power strengthens me for whatever challenges I may face today. If I feel sad or downhearted because the battles seem non-stop and relentless for a season, I'm greatly encouraged by the truth that God is in control of all things—past, present, and future. And I feel reassured that His mighty hand holds me, my family, and all those I love.

But perhaps most of all, our God is the One who has the power to give life to the lifeless. He alone has the power to raise the dead. He alone has the ability to sustain life—yours and mine.

So as we struggle to face our hard things today, we must call to our minds all that God has done in the past for us. We must learn to linger in the Scriptures and rest in His everlasting promises of redemption, restoration, and resurrection. As we ponder these great truths, the daily difficulties we face will shrink, and even diminish, in light of God's eternal greatness.

Today, when we are tempted to get bogged in the day's hardships and challenges, let's each choose to do an about-turn in our hearts and minds. Let's decide to view all of life through the lens of eternity.

One simple practice we can adapt is to ask ourselves if our current "hard thing" will even matter in eternity. Be honest. Will it? Or is our hard thing simply an inconvenience or a matter of inconsequence that simply feels big in the moment?

We have to learn to ask ourselves hard questions in this life. And we have to be willing to face our sinful tendency to complain over things that are non-issues in light of all eternity. God hates a grumbling tongue.

I pray that we each learn to focus on what is eternal, as God commands. As we obey Him in this, we will discover a supernatural joy that circumstances cannot diminish—for He never changes and our comfort and joy come from God's never-changing character.

This day and onward, let's discipline ourselves to think about the difficulties and disturbances of our lives through the lens of eternity. We will be blessed, and we will be changed.

My Heart's Cry

Father, I am coming to You feeling downhearted. It's been a challenging week and I feel ill-equipped to handle everything that is being thrown at me. Help me, Lord, to reframe all these difficulties and choose to view them in light of eternity. I know that as I immerse myself in the Scriptures, I walk away refreshed and renewed from within. Keep nudging me to run to You in prayer and to Your Word for truth and guidance. I know I need to become more disciplined in how I react and view the hard things in my life. You tell me to rejoice in all things and that the joy of the Lord will fill my heart. Give me the grace and the strength to obey You in this crucial area. Amen.

We Can Do Hard Things

1. *Find hope and help in God's past provision.* When you spend time alone with God today, ask Him to bring to your mind times when your life was especially difficult and yet you were reminded to view your hard things in light of eternity. Recall how changing perspective can change everything, even though circumstances may remain the same. Think about how God transforms even the greatest losses into something beautiful—in His time.

2. *Find hope and help in God's present provision.* As you consider today's hard things you face, ask God for the divine wisdom to view these challenges and hardships through the lens of eternity. Ask Him to show you how He has transformed past hardships—in His time. Pray for eyes to see and trust in God's wisdom and plans for you, even if nothing makes sense from your human perspective.
3. *Find hope and help in God's future provision.* Ask the Lord to help you focus upon His unchanging character as you contemplate the coming weeks. Ask God to continually reveal His intimate care and love for you. Pray for greater faith so the next time you face something extremely hard, you will lean into the loving arms of Christ. Meditate on passages that speak of eternity and how blessed we all will be once we are in God's presence for all time.

23

Never Stop Being a Learner

Therefore, since we are surrounded by such a great cloud of witnesses, let us throw off everything that hinders and the sin that so easily entangles. And let us run with perseverance the race marked out for us, fixing our eyes on Jesus, the pioneer and perfecter of faith. For the joy set before him he endured the cross, scorning its shame, and sat down at the right hand of the throne of God.

Hebrews 12:1–2

THE BIBLE IS full of emotionally evocative stories in which one person was reconciled with another. We love to applaud the wonderful ending of such tales.

However, in our own lives, we are called to reconcile in a variety of fashions, none of them easy. For instance, when a family member or a friend sins against us, it is hard to set aside our pain and grievance and offer forgiveness.

But this is what God calls us all to do. Jesus said to forgive "seventy-seven times"—meaning we are to have no limit to our forgiveness.

Another form that reconciliation takes is that of accepting the hard truth that as God's own beloved, chosen ones, we no longer have any rights to our lives. Christ paid the price for our sins. In other words, He bought us. We no longer belong to ourselves and, as Romans 12 states, we are to offer ourselves as living sacrifices to God, which is our reasonable service.

This truth could not be made any clearer. We are not our own.

Thus, we must reconcile the fact that what we expect God to do in our lives may not turn out as we anticipated, but we must surrender and submit in any case. This is a hard reconciliation. It is a difficult principle to accept and to learn.

We are no longer the masters of our lives; we are now servants to the Most High. As such, we must train ourselves to think in terms of eternity.

How so? Each choice we make should be sifted through the lens of Scripture. Every decision must be in alignment with the plumb line of God's Word. If we aren't certain about a specific choice before us, we go directly to the Bible and search its truths and principles. We seek the counsel of wise believers, and we seek to be learners.

What does a learner look like? What attributes constitute a learner that God accepts?

Humility. Teachableness. Sincerity. Purity of heart. Wisdom. Sensitivity to sin. A tender conscience. The pursuit of holiness. An obedient heart. A student of the Bible. One who prays and mediates upon Scripture. One who admits his or her sins and seeks forgiveness. All of these qualities make up the personhood of a genuine learner—a person who never stops learning.

So today, when you face hard decisions, choose to submit yourself, including your preferences and plans, to God. In humility, ask God to teach you the way you should go. And then do not balk at the path that God sets you on.

Learn the truth that God always knows best. His way is always high above what we can ask or think.

As you take on the posture of a learner, watch and see what God will do with the hard things in your life. And prepare to be amazed.

My Heart's Cry

Father, please speak comfort and hope to my heart. I am facing some difficult decisions, and I am not sure how to move forward. I want to obey You in all things and be submissive to Your perfect will, but right now, I'm struggling to understand what that even means. Give me Your heavenly wisdom and understanding. Clothe me with a humble and teachable heart. Show me my next steps and give me the grace to accept what is coming next, even if it isn't what I desire. Lord, I so need Your assurance and comfort today. I feel out of my depth with nowhere to turn but to You. Even as I pray, I know this is exactly where You want me to be—running straight to Your loving arms. Amen.

We Can Do Hard Things

1. *Find hope and help in God's past provision.* As you approach God's holy presence, be mindful of His glory, majesty, and goodness. Begin your time with Him not in petitions, but in praise and adoration. Then lay your requests before His feet, remembering how He led you, cared for you, and sustained you in the past. Thank Him for His perfect provision and learn to be a good rememberer. Wherever God has taken you in the past, know that it was for your good and His glory.
2. *Find hope and help in God's present provision.* When you get alone with God, ask Him to settle your restless heart and mind. Ask Him to bring you to a place of peace and inner calm. Pray that He will enable you to fix your mind on Him and not on your problems. Then pray with thanksgiving that you know God hears your every prayer, and He has

promised to lead you, teach you, and bring you safely home to heaven.

3. *Find hope and help in God's future provision.* If you are experiencing confusion about the future, and it is causing anxiety and worry, confess to the Lord your sin of doubt and unbelief. Tell the Lord everything you are worried about—everything that is tempting you to not trust in His plan for you. God waits for us to pour our hearts out before Him, and He will hear and answer our cries for help. Remember that the more swiftly we flee to God for protection, the more we are evidencing our growing faith in Him and learning to receive the comfort and care we so desire.

24

Difficulties: God's Opportunity to Prove Himself Faithful

God is our refuge and strength, an ever-present help in trouble. Therefore we will not fear, though the earth give way and the mountains fall into the heart of the sea, though its waters roar and foam and the mountains quake with their surging.

Psalm 46:1–3

AT THIS POINT in time, I am grieving each time I see my mom. She has been on a slow decline for some years, and recently it's become even more painful to watch her diminish and change both mentally and physically. Some days after an especially emotional visit, I cry out to the Lord and lament that my mom is no longer the mother I have known and loved.

Life is full of hard things. Aging is one of those hard, hard things we must reckon with in regard to our own bodies and others we love. We routinely joke about getting older and poke fun about forgetting details. But when it comes to how aging affects our relationships with our family and friends, it is just plain hard.

That being said, Psalm 46 has become one of my favorite go-to passages in Scripture since my mom's decline. I find great comfort in its words and the implications found throughout this entire psalm.

First and most important is the statement that God is my refuge. God is my strength. God is my ever-present help in time of trouble.

Let's unpack these important promises. God is where I go when I need to hide and feel sheltered from life's brutal onslaughts. God is the One who provides the grace and strength I require to keep showing up and serving those who are in need, even when it hurts me to see how much they suffer.

Finally, God is always with me. God never walks away from me. God never leaves me with my sadness and desperation. God and His love surround me.

Let's be honest. When our lives are full of hard things, it's easy to fall into a fearful state and stay there. But God tells me I don't need to be afraid. Ever. Even when the earth gives way or the mountains fall into the depths of the roaring, foaming sea. Even when the mountains shake and quake. I do not have to be afraid. Why?

Let's return to the prior verse, which tells me that God is my refuge and my strength and my ever-present help in time of trouble. And honestly, that's all any of us really need to know and to believe.

Since I've adopted this psalm as one to sit and meditate on with the Lord, I've discovered that when I close my eyes and picture an earthquake or tsunami, I feel the depths to which God will shelter and protect me. The next time you feel overwhelmed by grief or by the present hard thing in your life, close your eyes and bring to mind the images that this passage promises us.

Remind yourself that God is your refuge. He is your strength. He is your ever-present help. Then give thanks that truly your circumstances, as hard as they may be, cannot compare to the promises God gives for the comfort and strength He gives us.

My Heart's Cry

Father, here I am again, feeling sadness and grief over what was and can never be again. I know the more I focus on You and Your loving-kindness and faithfulness, the more settled in my heart I become. But my heart still aches for what we have lost. Please help me to view these hard times as fresh opportunities to watch You do amazing things. Open my eyes so that I see all You are accomplishing around me. I want to be consistently joyful, but this is a hard challenge. I need You to strengthen me and surround me with Your loving presence so I will be a blessing to others. Thank You for being my refuge, my strength, and my ever-present help in these trying times. Amen.

We Can Do Hard Things

1. *Find hope and help in God's past provision.* As you spend quiet time alone with God, purposefully remember His past goodness and faithfulness to you during times when you felt afraid and overwhelmed by life's hard things. Record in your journal all memories—large and small—of specific ways God became your refuge and your strength, and was present in your time of trouble.
2. *Find hope and help in God's present provision.* Today, sit in silence before the Lord and contemplate on the truth that He is God. Focus on His precious promises that He will be your refuge, your strength, and your ever-present help in time of trouble. Then meditate on the mental images the second part of this passage evokes. Consider the damaging power of an earthquake and a tsunami, and realized still God tells you to fear not, for He is with you.
3. *Find hope and help in God's future provision.* Ask God to help you see every hardship in your life as an opportunity to watch Him work on your behalf. Instead of dreading the future or

being afraid of what may happen next, take the faith-filled stance and praise God in advance for all He will do for you and on your behalf. Speak His promises to be your refuge, your strength, and your ever-present help in times of trouble. Then remind yourself daily of this passage. Realize it doesn't matter what happens around you if you find your shelter and security in God.

25

Embrace Laughter as a Perspective Booster

She is clothed with strength and dignity;
she can laugh at the days to come.

Proverbs 31:25

I HAVE A FRIEND who has the gift of laughter, if such a thing exists. She can bring a smile to the face of anyone in the room, simply by her presence. It is a wondrous blessing to behold.

She has a way of helping others see God's good hand of fatherly affection in everything. Whether it's a small blessing or a challenge of mammoth proportions, my friend has learned to open her eyes to really see. God has done such a beautiful work in my friend's life and it continually flows from her countenance.

I want to emulate this wise and winsome approach to life in all its varying shapes, sizes, shades, and configurations. But the question is, how do we so shift our negative thoughts and our long-ingrained habits so we can become like the woman in this passage in Proverbs, "She can laugh at the days to come"?

For in truth, a large portion of my own inability to view today's hard things well is because I routinely create a disastrous future in my mind's eye. I often create a mental picture of what-ifs that takes me under emotionally because I begin piling one hard thing upon another until they all topple over, along with my spirit and courage.

Not only is this sinful pattern of responding to hard things wrong, it has a negative impact on everyone around me. I've been learning that God wants me to not only read His Word, pray, and meditate upon His Scriptures, He wants me to obey those hard-to-follow commands like Philippians 4:8. For when I begin to pray and think through this list of mercies and blessings, I have to submit my will first to God and then move to being truly thankful for His sovereign plan in my life.

Yes, we can all learn to view the future with a robust and hopeful outlook. But the deeper principle must fill our hearts and minds. We must place ourselves rightly as bondservants that are under God's rule. And we must constantly be mindful that our Creator and Father has the right to do with us, and everything that concerns us, as He wishes.

And He will do so. Thank Him for that, for in our limited mindset we cannot know what is best for us or those we love.

Truly, you and I can learn to see all of life through the lens of possibility because we have a heavenly Father who created us, chose us, saved us, and is daily redeeming us and growing us into the image of our Savior, the Lord Jesus Christ.

This current work of sanctification will never end this side of heaven. I believe the quicker we understand and accept this hard truth, the better for us and everyone around us. For it will affect how we respond to hard things today, tomorrow, and every day until we meet Jesus face-to-face.

Again, hard things are a part of everyday life on earth. But Jesus has given us all that we need to grow into the kind of believer that really sees God's good hand of provision, protection, and plan in every situation. Let's thank Him today for the gift that never diminishes: our eternal salvation and ultimate destination—heaven.

My Heart's Cry

Father, I come to You this morning full of fear and trepidation. I woke up and immediately my thoughts went to all the people in my life who are suffering. There is nothing more that I desire than to take away all the hard things in their lives right now. But even as I utter those words I realize how wrong I am to think this way. All throughout Scripture You remind us that we will face hardship, suffering, grief, and loss. I know this. So why do I continue to be surprised when suffering knocks on my door and affects my loved ones? Please transform the way I think about these challenges and hardships. Keep reminding me that You are doing a work of eternal proportions in all of us and that You use suffering to accomplish this goal. Thank You for Your patience with me as I wrestle through all these hard things and help me, Lord, to deepen my trust in You and You alone. Amen.

We Can Do Hard Things

1. *Find hope and help in God's past provision.* When you awaken each day, prioritize time spent in God's Word and prayer. Rather than checking your phone or emails, start the day connecting with God first. As you sit alone with Him, ask the Lord to bring to your mind times when you felt overwhelmed by life but God met your need for encouragement through another believer. Ask God to help you become an encourager for someone else today.
2. *Find hope and help in God's present provision.* As you contemplate your current list of hard things, ask the Lord to begin helping you to reframe every difficulty into an opportunity to watch Him work in a mighty way. Pray that God will open your eyes to see, really see, His good hand of fatherly love in each situation. Then ask God to help you to retrain the way you see life's trials and to learn to view

them as instruments in His mighty hand to sanctify and purify you.

3. *Find hope and help in God's future provision.* Today, when you think about the unknown future, ask God to give you His grace, strength, and a robust faith that seeks to trust Him, come what may. Ask the Lord to begin right now to help you reframe your fears and worries into a mindset of knowing that everything is possible with God. Purpose to grow into the kind of believer who truly does laugh at the future because you know that God holds it all in His loving, faithful hands.

26

Unite Efforts with Other Believers and Be Amazed

Look at the nations and watch—and be utterly amazed. For I am going to do something in your days that you would not believe, even if you were told.

Habakkuk 1:5

WHEN WE DECIDE to let other believers join us in the battles of life, everything can shift. For aren't we all prone to want to fight through hardships and daily challenges in our own solitary ways?

We don't often want to bring others into situations that feel overwhelming and frightening to us. We would rather endure the worst while making a valiant attempt to conquer in our own strength. But I wonder if this isn't exactly where Satan wants us to tread: alone and vulnerable to any type of attack—spiritual or otherwise.

As members in a family of believers worldwide, we don't have any excuses for being lone Christians living a life of solitude. Certainly, we all need time alone. We can thrive when we get alone and seek the Lord without outside distractions.

And still, God has wired us to need one another. From the very beginning of creation, God said it was not good for Adam to dwell alone. We need people in our lives and they need us—no exceptions exist.

We have another very good reason to unite efforts with fellow believers for the sake of the kingdom work. God often places us in situations in which we cannot succeed without the combined efforts of others who unite for a common cause.

Consider the biblical characters who won battles and conquered kingdoms. They didn't do it alone. Each harrowing tale speaks of God's supernatural enabling and guidance, as well the obedience and united effort of His chosen people. God gives us a hard work to do, and He expects us to submit and obey His plan. And generally, this requires team effort to succeed.

Again, this is where the safety and security of a group of God-followers seeking wholeheartedly after Him can make all the difference. When we are caught in a battle for survival, our tendency is to grow weary, become discouraged, and give up. This is especially true when we attempt hard things in our own strength and on our own.

But when we unite with other like-minded Christians and join together to complete a task or overcome a difficult challenge, everything changes. We don't have to rely solely upon ourselves because we have an entire team of individuals upon whom to lean and be strengthened.

As this passage in Habakkuk tells us, look at the nations and watch—be amazed because God will do something in your time that you wouldn't even believe if someone told you. When we seek to serve God along with fellow Christians, we are in the best company. For we can strengthen and support each other, lean on and shore up one another, press on and urge each other on, and we can steady the unstable and lend a good word of encouragement to the despondent.

Only when we are in the company of other believers can we overcome the hard obstacles and impossible challenges God sets before us. Instead of stubbornly taking the path of solitude, let's each ask God to supply us with a group of Christian battle-ready compatriots to join us in our spiritual and worldly endeavors. We can then truly watch and see what God will do—and be amazed.

My Heart's Cry

Father, I am struggling again on my own trying to fulfill the tasks You have given me. I don't know why I'm such a slow learner. I never want to ask others for assistance even when I know they are willing to step in and help. Please Lord, help me to understand the wisdom of joining with others to serve You. Clothe me with a humble and teachable heart that willingly seeks support from other believers and accepts their help. Show me the wisdom of joining with others as a way to offer and get the needed support everyone requires. I am Yours, and I want to serve You wherever You send me, Father. Open my eyes, and let me see where You are directing me. Amen.

We Can Do Hard Things

1. *Find hope and help in God's past provision.* As you reflect on the past, ask the Lord to remind you of those seasons when you felt alone and overwhelmed. Ask Him if you were then willing to allow others to join with you to help. Be honest with yourself and ask the Lord to give you wisdom and a willingness to gather with other believers in the future as He tasks you with any new hard things in the coming weeks and months.
2. *Find hope and help in God's present provision.* When you contemplate all that you need to accomplish today, ask yourself if you would be better equipped if you enlisted others to join you in your tasks. Ask the Lord to provide support from fellow believers. Then pray about whom you should ask to join you in your responsibilities as needed.

Remind yourself that work is lightened when many hands set upon a job together.

3. *Find hope and help in God's future provision.* Take time to pray about the coming weeks and months, and ask God to give you wisdom and understanding about where and what you should become involved in regarding service. Ask the Lord to give you a group of like-minded believers to work with and to open doors of opportunity for you to serve together. Then begin a campaign of daily prayer for this request until God makes His will clear to you. Never forget the value of joining forces with others to accomplish God's good and perfect will for you.

27

Equip Yourself with Prayer and Praise

Is anyone among you suffering? Let him pray. Is anyone cheerful? Let him sing praise.

James 5:13, ESV

WHEN I WAS A newer believer, I loved listening to Christian music and attending Christian concerts. My husband and I spent many evenings enjoying the worship music from a variety of musicians.

As we had our children, they loved the same music, and it often filled our home. Today, as empty nesters, I realized that I rarely play music in our home anymore. Instead, I have opted to listen to podcasts on Bible exposition.

Recently, my husband asked me what I was listening to and I mentioned the pastor I was hearing teach on the book of Luke. Then he looked at me and asked why I don't ever listen to worship music anymore. I stopped and asked myself the same question.

Why? Well, I've learned that much in the evangelical music industry is not theologically sound. Not one to give up that easily, my husband informed me that he had a terrific playlist he would share with me.

Now, as I've gotten back into listening to and worshipping the Lord through music, I realized something important. I never should have given up listening and praising the Lord through music. Sure, I had a good reason for opting out of some performers' work. But as my husband pointed out, other groups were biblically sound and do elevate God in every song they produce.

My wise spouse also was trying to get me to understand how powerful music is in our spiritual lives when it does what it is meant to do—praise and elevate the Lord. I had forgotten how powerful uplifting music can be playing in the background of our home.

Then I began remembering. I thought of specific hard seasons in our parenting years when we had no obvious solutions to our children's problems and how simply hearing worship music lifted my eyes back toward heaven and the Lord. How could have I forgotten these precious times?

Honestly, one of the most valuable Christian practices we can adopt is to pray and praise God. We all know it's essential to spend time daily in God's Word and to pray, but do we spend as much thought on praising God?

When we deliberately pair prayer and praise, our hard things diminish in size. We come to our loving heavenly Father with our adoration, our confessions, our thanksgiving, and our supplications. Why not spend more time throughout our days and nights in adoration, expressing itself through praise and worship.

None of us needs a grand singing voice, I certainly do not have one. But every one of us needs to take more seriously the countless psalms that command us to offer our praise and worship to God. What simpler way to fulfill this command than to select God-worthy music and let its message permeate our homes and lives?

So today, when you feel the hard things of life closing in on you, turn up the praise music. Then tune in to prayer and praise combined, and watch how God lifts you above your hard circumstances and into His holy presence.

My Heart's Cry

Father, everything around me seems so dark and dismal. I keep recounting all those who are hurting and suffering in my mind. It's as though I have this "on" switch in my brain that never stops recycling all the hard things happening around me. Please, Lord, help me to change my focus from discouragement and defeat to praise and thanksgiving. I have neglected to offer You the worship You so rightly deserve; please forgive me. When I keep my eyes on You, all the hard things in life diminish, and I can see clearly again. This life with all of its woes is nothing compared to the joy we will experience when we meet Jesus face-to-face. Amen.

We Can Do Hard Things

1. *Find hope and help in God's past provision.* Remember seasons in your life when you were consistently praying and praising God. Remember how it helped you to shift your focus from your hard circumstances to God and all His glory. Remind yourself how God changed you from the inside when you focused on Him. Then thank Him anew for these times of praise and worship.
2. *Find hope and help in God's present provision.* Today as you set aside time to be with God alone, consider how you apportion your time to praise and worship. Honestly assess how much you truly desire to praise God for who He is and what He has done. Prayerfully ask the Lord to help you to spend more of your hours in adoration and worship. Purpose to change any habits in your life that hinder you from focusing on Him, beginning right now.
3. *Find hope and help in God's future provision.* As you ponder the future and all its unknowns, ask God to give you the wisdom and understanding to face any future hard things by being

prepared spiritually. Ask God to help you understand how a heart full of praise and thanksgiving is a heart prepared for hard things. Let God show you that a humble and submissive heart is prepared for hard things. Then spend some time in quiet with the Lord, listening to praise and worship music with the thought in mind that God is, and always will be, in control of everything that concerns you and your future.

28

Know that God Will Never Disappoint

Anyone who trusts in him will never be disappointed.

Romans 10:11, NCV

TODAY I SAT WITH a young woman who is battling several debilitating illnesses that—barring a miracle—will always be part of her earthly body. There is no cure or an end date to her suffering on this planet, and she knows it. As the beautiful fall sunshine streamed through the windows of her home, I noted small but significant signs of God's blessing on her life despite the physical suffering she faces every day.

In each room, I noticed lovely Scripture-embossed, wooden frames adorning the walls. I spotted family photos in vibrant colors, which reminded me that this young woman was loved and cherished. Flowers from her garden graced the table. A fragrant candle on the counter glowed and emitted a warming scent. Everywhere I looked, I realized I was witnessing God's good hand of tender care upon this woman.

Yes, this suffering woman is hurting with pain I can't imagine. She has maladies that often hinder her from doing her daily tasks.

She doesn't sleep well because of her conditions, so she frequently fights exhaustion all day. And yet, when she speaks of her life and her obvious limitations, she isn't bitter. She doesn't rail against God. She isn't disappointed. Amazing.

Her life is hard in so many different ways but it has colored her perspective in a beautifully supernatural way. As we talked about her hopes for the future, she admitted she has had to temper her goals and be realistic about her dreams. But even so, there was no hint of self-pity or remorse. God, she told me, has been teaching her to trust Him completely, and He has been giving her the grace to do so.

Day by day, my friend has been learning that God is good, and what He does is good—that includes giving her a body that continually battles illness. The work He is doing inside of her heart is where the real treasure is to be found.

God, she says, is transforming her from the inside out, and yes, she admits, it's a hard, hard work. But it's also worth the pain she has endured for she knows God in a way she never would have without her life-altering ailments. He has become her everything. Amazing.

She has come to accept that God has a plan for her that she may never fully understand this side of heaven, but still she knows that His way is best. What was once a season of deep disappointment has been transformed into a sweet and settled acceptance and inner peace.

In the same way that I saw all the external marks of beauty within her home—visual reminders of God's intimate care for her—she knows God is working out a beautiful transformation on the inside of her soul, unseen to others but seen by God.

I left this suffering young woman with a heart full of wonder and thankfulness. I prayed as I drove away that God would never let me forget her faithful example of a woman who has surrendered her all to her loving heavenly Father, one day at a time.

I hope that I, too, learn that no matter how hard my life is, I know that God is good and what He does is good—the difficulties are all for my good and His glory. I pray that we all learn that we are in the safest position ever when we place the full weight of our trust in God—not in our human wisdom and finite understanding. For when we fall into His loving arms and embrace His perfect plan for us, we discover there is no room for disappointment, for He will fill our hearts with love, joy, and peace for all eternity.

My Heart's Cry

Father, I witnessed something today that I can't shake off. I don't want to forget the beautiful reminder of what I saw in another's suffering. I was expecting to offer comfort and support to this hurting friend, and just the opposite occurred. She encouraged me. She showed me how to live in the hardest seasons imaginable with love, joy, and peace. Lord, I was amazed and humbled by her unwavering trust in You. Her words were not complaint or of disappointment. Rather, she spoke of Your goodness and grace. Please help me to grow into this maturity of spirit and to learn to trust You as she has done. What a blessing she was to me; what a challenge her life is to me. Help me, Lord. Amen.

We Can Do Hard Things

1. *Find hope and help in God's past provision.* This morning as you open your Bible, spend some time in Psalms and read through several chapters, taking note of the story each psalm tells. Examine how the writer expresses sorrow, grief, anger, and disappointment in life and circumstances. Then look for resolution within each psalm. Note how after the psalmist cries out to God, he then finds love, joy, peace with God, and God's plan for his life. Ask God to help you work

through any past disappointments that continue to bring you pain, and pray for the grace and power to trust Him with your life.

2. *Find hope and help in God's present provision.* Today, as you study God's Word, be mindful of the powerful, active, and living Word that God has given to change you from the inside out. Pray that God would bring illumination and understanding about any present hardships you face and that He would remind you to see all of life through the lens of eternity. Then, thank Him for loving you in such an intimate and personal way as He sends new-morning blessings each day as a reminder of this love.
3. *Find hope and help in God's future provision.* When thoughts of the future invade your heart and mind, tempting you to worry and fret, ask God to bring to your mind His past provisions for you. Pray that God would show you how He has cared for you in the past, loved and provided for you today, and has promised to meet your every need for all your tomorrows. Then spend time in praise and worship as you mediate on God's unchanging, unwavering character of holiness, goodness, and faithfulness.

29

God Is Always Orchestrating Good on Our Behalf

The heavens proclaim the glory of God.
The skies display his craftsmanship.

Psalm 19:1, NLT

A WHILE BACK, A pastor said something about suffering in this hard world. We were talking about a mutual friend who had endured an extremely tough childhood and continues to be affected by this trauma.

The pastor pointed out that everyone has bruises from his or her past. Everyone.

This brief, powerful statement caught me up short, and I nodded in agreement. He is absolutely right. We all have bruises; some are simply more hidden than others.

As we contemplate our own childhoods, our families of origin, and our growing up years, we can all point out specific areas of weakness or sinful tendencies that were part of our home lives. The stain of sin runs through our world and our families and will continue to be the unseen battle we fight until we see Jesus face-to-face.

Some people might argue that those who grew up in Christian families might be exempt from such bruises. But it isn't so.

Individuals from believing and unbelieving families alike struggle against a common enemy: our unseen but powerful foe, Satan, and his demons. But a tremendous difference lies in how we Christians face our foes and deal with our bruises. We have the God of the universe as our heavenly Father; Jesus, His Son, as our Savior; and the Holy Spirit abiding within us as our comforter and guide through this life.

Much of life is hard. Perhaps even more true: Life can be hard to understand. But when we learn to orient our hearts toward what God is doing all around us, everything changes.

Think about this passage from Psalm 19, which tells us to look and see that the heavens proclaim God's glory and the skies, His craftsmanship. God has given us signs in nature that tell us who He is and what He values.

Nature in all of its beautiful diversity and colorful splendor speaks to us of our Father's attention to detail, His appreciation of beauty, His creativity, and His display of multi-dimensional wonder. Nature is one of God's good gifts to us because He displays His supernatural and powerful ability to orchestrate everything on earth and in the heavens. God does indeed orchestrate everything for our ultimate good, Scripture tell us this is true.

Our part is to learn to see God's good hand of orchestration in our lives—every single day. On those blissfully, happy mountaintop days, see His hand in the day, and give Him thanks.

On those dismal, down-in-the-valley-and-can't-get-out days, see His hand in it, and give Him thanks. We must learn to see, really see, God's strong hand of reigning sovereignty in each day and every hour.

The more we train ourselves to see past the brokenness and the bruises we all carry, we can become free from the inside out. Our focus throughout our hours and days must continually look toward Christ and refuse to fuel the fire of our hard circumstances. When we truly believe that God is doing a good work today—in us and all around us—we rise above our hard things and give thanks and glory to God.

Today, when you next feel tempted to ask God "why" for the umpteenth time, choose instead to say "thank You." Thank God for the world of wonder that proclaims His glory and the skies that speak of His unsurpassed craftsmanship. It's all about leaning in, drawing close, becoming intimate, and fully surrendering ourselves to Him, the Creator of all.

My Heart's Cry

Father, thank You for the glorious splendor that is evident all around me. Help me to remember to take time every day to walk among Your created world and to take note of everything You have made for our benefit and blessing. Lord, open my eyes to see past the brokenness and the bruises from my past. Give me Your divine wisdom to see Your loving hand of orchestration in every moment of my days. Thank You, Father, for creating me, for calling me, for saving me, and for sustaining me until I see Jesus face-to-face. Amen.

We Can Do Hard Things

1. *Find hope and help in God's past provision.* Take time this week to quietly reflect about your past. Ask God to help you better see and understand His good hand of loving care and protection, even in those hard times. Pray that God reveals to you how He has used your brokenness and your bruises to help you mature and become more like Jesus. Then spend time in praise and thanksgiving for His daily reminders of His perfect love toward you.
2. *Find hope and help in God's present provision.* As you gather with the Lord today, pray that He would help you to see the grandeur and glory of the created world all around you. Ask

God to bring understanding to your heart and mind about how nature reveals God's love to us as His children. Then make plans to get outdoors, no matter what the weather, and take a prayer walk, praising God with each step you take. Thank Him for these constant reminders of His powerful majesty and strength to hold creation together by the Word of His power.

3. *Find hope and help in God's future provision.* Set aside time to be prayerful and mindful about your past, present, and future. Ask the Lord to open your mind to remember how He has always met your every need and how He always hears your every prayer. Ask God to bring understanding and insight about how He has transformed your pain and your hard things into something beautiful to behold in your ever-growing maturity and character. Then thank Him for orchestrating both the small and the large in your life for your good and His glory.

30

It's All for Our Good and His Glory

And we know that in all things God works for the good of those who love him, who have been called according to his purpose. For those God foreknew he also predestined to be conformed to the image of his Son, that he might be the firstborn among many brothers and sisters. And those he predestined, he also called; those he called, he also justified; those he justified, he also glorified.

Romans 8:28–30

THIS SCRIPTURE PASSAGE is so well-known and so often quoted that it has become far too familiar and far too misunderstood. We have all read this passage when we are in hard places and hard seasons when nothing seems to be going well.

We scour through the Bible in search of specific passages that will encourage us, give us fresh hope, and shore us up to rise in the morning and start again.

So it makes sense why so many of us camp out in Romans 8 and plead with God to help us make sense of the trials in our lives.

We so want to believe that our faithful heavenly Father will issue a rescue-mission command, and we will be transported out of the sticky, painful, and dismal circumstances we are mired in. And sometimes God does do this—He does initiate a rescue mission of sorts on our behalf.

Then during other times our circumstances do not change, the pressure does not lighten up, and we constantly fight an uphill battle one day at a time. This is our lives in general—for most of our days. But I believe in the face of this hard truth that God frequently does not erase our hardships—they may even escalate—but God wants us to see the bigger picture and the deeper principle at play.

As we read this passage in Romans 8, the writer tells us several important truths. First, God does indeed work to transform everything (the good and the bad) into something good for those who belong to Him. That's a fact.

Second fact—God is simultaneously sanctifying us so that we mature and become image bearers of His Son, Jesus. These two facts may at times appear to contradict each other but they do not.

The rub we feel between these two objectives is that we don't understand why God is orchestrating our lives as He does. And He will do so at His good pleasure because He is God, and He has that right. And as humans, we are always attempting to make sense of our lives. We are experts at asking "why," rather than humbly trusting and submitting to God's always-perfect plan for us.

One of the greatest obstacles for us to overcome when we are in a hard place is understanding that God often has placed us in this precarious position for a single reason—so we have to recognize how much we need Him for every breath we take.

As we look at our lives—the good and the hard—we must be willing to ask if there are any areas in which we are truly relying on God to fulfill His command. Many believers have so sequestered themselves into comfortable lives that they don't do anything that requires God's help.

So what does God do? He sovereignly positions us in hard places so we can only look to Him for rescue. And He does rescue us. But God's form of rescue looks very different than what we might envision.

God's form of rescue may come in the form of giving more grace and strength, building our trust and faith, or even developing humility and submission. God will tailor His rescue team to fit our spiritual needs.

Truly, everything God allows to touch our lives is for our ultimate good and His glory. The good and the hard will work together to transform us from immature, selfish believers into mature, selfless Christians who are Christ's image bearers to a dying world. And isn't that the best news of all?

My Heart's Cry

Father, hold me close today. I so desperately need Your loving touch. I have tried to face so many obstacles that are far bigger and stronger than I am. Somehow, I thought I could handle the challenges and the stress that would come. I was wrong. Lord, help me to lean on You for what I require today. Only You can provide the hope and strength I need to walk through this day. Help me to have the wisdom to trust You, to submit to You, and to serve You in whatever capacity You lead me. You are all I have, and that is all I need. Amen.

We Can Do Hard Things

1. *Find hope and help in God's past provision.* Take the time you need to reflect upon God's past provision for you. Ask the Lord to help you to remember specific times, events, and circumstances when you felt nothing good was happening in your life.

Then thank Him, as you start to recall His intimate hand of care and provision for you. Praise Him for His wondrous love and His persistent work of sanctification in your life.

2. *Find hope and help in God's present provision.* Ask the Lord to bring to your mind today any hard decisions, hard work, or hard relationships that have worried you. Then thank God in advance for the provision He promises you each day. Praise Him for the transforming work of sanctification that He will do in your life as He uses these hard things to make you into an image bearer of Jesus.
3. *Find hope and help in God's future provision.* Think about the coming months and years, and ask the Lord to give you the grace and strength to face whatever you need in your process of sanctification. Pray boldly. Ask great things of our great God. Then thank Him for His ongoing work in your life and for His ability to see clearly what you will become in the years to come. Praise Him, for He is worthy of all your worship and thanksgiving.

CLC
PUBLICATIONS
Fort Washington, PA 19034

This book was published by CLC Publications, an outreach of CLC Ministries International. The purpose of CLC is to make evangelical Christian literature available to all nations so that people may come to faith and maturity in the Lord Jesus Christ. This book has [illegible]

[illegible]

WWW.[illegible]

To know more about [illegible] of the founding [illegible] CLC International [illegible] to read

[illegible]

Fight for Joy

Discovering Peace in Impossible Circumstances

A Devotional by

Michele Howe

When Your Enemy Is Despair—Fight for Joy!

What do you do when you find yourself deep in heartache, pain, or confusion? Where do you turn when life feels out of control and your foundations are shaken?

Michele Howe has been there—facing cancer, family grief, and waves of personal and relational hardship, she discovered that joy was not out of reach but was a promise worth fighting for.

In *Fight for Joy*, Michele invites you into her journey through pain to the unshakable hope of God's presence. With tender honesty, biblical wisdom, prayers, and practical steps, she shows how you can:

- Reframe your pain through God's eternal perspective
- Experience peace that thrives in impossible situations
- Take small, faithful steps toward healing when you feel paralyzed
- Rest in God's daily mercies—no matter what tomorrow holds

Join Michele and enter into the fray as you *Fight for Joy* today!

Size 5¼ x 8, Pages 132

ISBN: 978-1-61958-413-6
ISBN (*e-book*): 978-1-61958-419-8

PRAISE!

A DOOR TO GOD'S PRESENCE

"I will extol the LORD at all times;
his praise will always be on my lips."

(Psalm 34:1)

Do you practice praising God? God deserves all our praise! But what is the importance of praise in the life of a Christian? How can praise deepen our relationship with God? What does godly, biblical, and God-honoring praise look like? What does Scripture say about praise?

Warren and Ruth Myers call on each Christian to cultivate a deeper relationship with God through the daily practice of rich praise.

Warren and Ruth showcase the biblical foundation for praise and invite you to enter the true joy and freedom of praising our glorious God.

Discover how to praise the Lord in spirit and truth in ***Praise!***

Includes a one-week devotional study on praise

Size 5¼ x 8, Pages 185
ISBN: 978-1-61958-386-3
ISBN (*e-book*): 978-1-61958-389-4

PRAY!

HOW TO BE EFFECTIVE IN PRAYER

"Lord, teach us to pray."

(Luke 11:1)

God loves when His people pray! But just how important is prayer in a Christian's life? What should we pray about? Does God care how often we pray or what we pray for?

In this book, Warren and Ruth Myers teach us how to pray, outlining the biblical principles, patterns, and practices of prayer. They offer a rich theology of prayer, but also provide practical ways to enrich your prayer life. Whether helping you shape habits for your own quiet time or explaining the Lord's Prayer, Warren and Ruth use Scripture as the foundation for their teaching. They exhort all Christians to practice prayer, dependent on the help of the Holy Spirit, to intercede for the lost and support God's global mission.

Learn how to pray, whom to pray for, and why prayer matters.

Includes prayer-based tips for planning your quiet time

Size 5 1/4 x 8, Pages 211
ISBN: 978-1-61958-387-0
ISBN (*e-book*): 978-1-61958-388-7

DAILY THOUGHTS ON HOLINESS

Andrew Murray

This compilation of daily devotional readings emphasizes the focuses of Andrew Murray's writing and preaching—holiness and the deepening of the spiritual life. These bite-sized reflections will lead you in a day-to-day development of a holy life.

Paperback
Size $4^{1}/_{4}$ x 7, Pages 374
ISBN: 978-1-936143-48-1
IBSN (*e-book*): 978-1-61958-015-2

THE NORMAL CHRISTIAN LIFE

. . . is Watchman Nee's great Christian classic unfolding the central theme of "Christ our Life." Nee reveals the secret of spiritual strength and vitality that should be the normal experience of every Christian.

Trade paper ISBN: 978-0-87508-990-4

THE NORMAL CHRISTIAN LIFE STUDY GUIDE

This guide gives a brief summary of each chapter of the book and then gives questions designed to provoke thought and possible discussion.

Trade paper ISBN: 978-1-61958-129-6